Praise for

SAMMY HAGAR'S
COCKTAIL HITS

"I've spent many nights with Sambo in Cabo, Vegas, his house, my house…The guy knows how to shake it up in more ways than one!"

TOBY KEITH

"The Red Rocker has done it again. My friend sure knows his way around the bar! Delicious!"

CHEF EMERIL LAGASSE

"Sammy's palate is mesmerizing. He can tell you what's in a cocktail or the varietals of a wine he's never tasted before. He has a natural gift that leaves you speechless!"

LUCA GARAVOGLIA, CHAIRMAN, CAMPARI GROUP

"I've tasted Sammy's cocktails many times at my restaurant. It's difficult to keep him out from behind the bar!"

CHEF MICHAEL MINA

"Over the years, Sammy has acquired and used extensive knowledge of spirits to create his fabulous brands and cocktails! Terrific job, Sammy!"

JOHN PAUL DEJORIA, FOUNDER, PATRÓN SPIRITS

"I've been appreciating Sammy's spirits and cocktails for nearly two decades. His knowledge and passion shine in every glass!"

BOB CABRAL, JAMES BEARD AWARD–WINNING WINEMAKER

SAMMY HAGAR'S
COCKTAIL HITS

85 PERSONAL FAVORITES FROM THE RED ROCKER

SAMMY HAGAR & JAMES O. FRAIOLI

FOREWORD BY GUY FIERI

Cocktail Photography by **TUCKER + HOSSLER**

Lifestyle Photography by **LEAH STEIGER**

Skyhorse Publishing

Culinary Book Creations

Creative Director: James O. Fraioli
Designer: Jen Montgomery
Editor: Nicole Frail
Production Manager: James O. Fraioli

skyhorsepublishing.com; culinarybookcreations.com

10 9 8 7 6 5 4 3 2

Library of Congress Cataloging-in-Publication Data is available on file.

Print ISBN: 978-1-5107-6929-8
Ebook ISBN: 978-1-5107-6955-7

Printed in China

To all my fans who've supported everything I do—from my records, concerts, restaurants, spirits, charity events…the list goes on. I decided to write this book from all my experiences and pass it on to you, my Redheads, who've come along with me on this long, fun journey. This book should make it easier for y'all to throw your own party with your family and friends when I'm not available. I sincerely love you all.

Now, let's get this party started!
Cheers!

TABLE OF CONTENTS

FOREWORD BY GUY FIERI

Ever since I was a teenager, my amigo, partner, and spiritual advisor, Sammy Hagar, has been shouting at the top of his lungs, teaching me the ways of the world. I'd barely just gotten my license when he taught me that "I Can't Drive 55." And while growing up, I thought I had some pretty good swagger, but I learned quickly that "There's Only One Way to Rock." And of course, most importantly, when in doubt, you need "Mas Tequila." And here we are today, and the Red Rocker is going a step further, releasing *Sammy Hagar's Cocktail Hits*, eighty-five personal recipes that you're gonna dig. Let me tell you, this book is going to number one with a bullet.

But we haven't always been close buddies. I was just a local Northern California chef and restaurateur who really wanted to meet and hang out with the Red Rocker, so when I heard that he was having a tequila sales contest to win some backstage passes, I was all in. I sold more Cabo Wabo than anyone else in Nor Cal at what was then my very first restaurant, Johnny Garlic's, and next thing I knew, we were hanging out backstage at one of his shows. And so began a great friendship that has turned into much more.

Years down the road, when Sammy asked me to join forces with him in his newest tequila venture, Santo, it was a dream come true. To work side by side with a rock icon, serial entrepreneur, and truly, the godfather of premium tequila, is a chance of a lifetime. This guy can play for an entire stadium or mix you up a helluva margarita one-on-one and, in both cases, you feel like you're the only one in the room and you're getting the best of the best.

So, I've been lucky enough to befriend one of my idols and yes, it's everything you'd imagine. Whether it's sharing a great meal (he can cook, too!), talking about a song he wrote, or gettin' dirty in the agave fields of Jalisco, I always pay attention to make sure I don't miss a minute. But one of the greatest things about Sammy is how he loves to share all of these experiences with his friends, family, and fans, and this book is a perfect example of that. So, get your drinkin' shoes on because the Red Rocker has laid out all the cocktail hits and you're not gonna want to miss any of them.

*Love, Peace
& Taco Grease,*

Guy

INTRODUCTION

Hey, there. It's Sammy Hagar, best known as the former frontman of the iconic band Van Halen. My fans know me as the Red Rocker and as the songwriter behind hits like "I Can't Drive 55," "Right Now," and "Why Can't This Be Love." I couldn't be prouder of the success I've had in the music industry—winning a Grammy, being inducted into the Rock & Roll Hall of fame, creating songs that people know all around the world. But music is just one of my passions.

I'm also a businessman, a connoisseur of great cocktails, and the creator of Cabo Wabo Tequila, Sammy's Beach Bar Rums, and—along with my good friend and celebrity restaurateur Guy Fieri—a line of Santo Tequilas and Mezquila. I always figured if I could bring together great music, delicious cocktails, and people I care about, then I'm living the lifestyle I've always wanted. And that's what I'm sharing with you through the pages of *Sammy's Hagar's Cocktail Hits: 85 Personal Favorites from the Red Rocker*.

I created Cabo Wabo Cantinas and Sammy's Beach Bar & Grills so people could hang out with their friends and families, have a few drinks, laugh, and enjoy the good times and unique cultures of the places I enjoy most—and the recipes reflect those differences. Hawaii's slowed-down, low-stress island vibe. Mexico's friendly come-as-you-are spirit. Las Vegas's twenty-four-hour thrill-seeking energy,

and Hollywood's eclectic, glamorous scene.

First, we'll start with some bartending basics: how to set up your home bar, what liquors and glassware to have on hand, and the techniques you'll need to know when mixing up the cocktails in each chapter. Once you're set up, you'll be able to bring Hawaii's laid-back lifestyle into your home in a compilation I call *A Splash of Aloha!* They're Hawaii's coolest cocktails; many from Sammy's Beach Bar & Grill. They're shaken or stirred and served up with tropical flair. To help me out, I've enlisted the expertise of coauthor and James Beard Award-winner James O. Fraioli, who has a number of beautiful cocktail and culinary books under his belt.

All you need to feel like you're soaking up the sun on a tropical vacation is a few of these smooth cocktails loaded with island flavors: a frothy Coconut Mojito, an intriguing Hana Reviver, a sweet Maui Mama, a creamy Pineapple Piña Colada, a tempting Shark Bite, or a citrusy Tiki Swizzle. Enjoy these classics made new while poolside, inside, or outside on your sun-kissed patio. They're perfect for happy hours, summer barbecues, leisurely afternoons, or for creating a slice of paradise any day of the week, any place in the world.

In the next chapter, we'll venture down the coast of Baja to bring the flavors of Mexico into your home through my favorite South-of-the-Border cocktails. I call this compilation

Mas Tequila. When you're craving drinks that emphasize spiciness, vivaciousness, strength, and variation, flip straight to this list. They're drinks to liven up any fiesta or holiday. Los Cabos, Mexico, is all about the tastes of tequila and mezcal infused with music, culture, and carefree nightlife. Create the same mood in your home as I step behind the bar with you, serving up salty, spicy concoctions straight from my Cabo Wabo Mexico Cantina.

Try an epic Blanco Gimlet, Coco Loco, Coronarita, or a Mango Peño. Liven up the night with a vibrant Desert Pear Margarita, a lovely Guava Martini, or savor the old-world flavors of my refreshing Sangria. I've also included Guy Fieri and my go-to's: our smoky-laden Santo Oaxaca, Santa Paloma, and Santo Sunrise. Every drink from the other side of the Rio Grande is approachable and delicious; ingredients are easy to find, no matter where you live. In your home bar, like mine in Cabo San Lucas, the party never ends.

From Mexico, we'll touch down in Sin City, home to world-famous clubs and lounges, bottle service, and all-night dancing. You've heard the stories and seen all the hype; now, in a compilation I call *Sinful Signatures*, I'll bring that velvet-rope experience right to you. When you want to drink like a Vegas local, these are your cocktails—even if you're hundreds of miles from the Strip. No dress codes, long lines, and crowded tables to contend with; we'll turn your home into a swanky VIP venue brimming with my greatest cocktail hits from Cabo Wabo Las Vegas and Sammy's Beach Bar & Grill Las Vegas. Enjoy drinks

with a flair that echoes the showmanship and flavor of Vegas: my voluptuous Brazilian Kiss, dance-on-the-table Cabo Rockin' Iced Tea, an elegant Kir Royale, and the berry-infused Vojito. It's a sinful array of tempting drinks that are easy to make and sure to please.

Finally, we'll wrap things up in Hollywood with a compilation called *Tinseltown Twists with Cleveland Pre-Funk.* Cleveland is home to another Sammy's Beach Bar & Grill as well as the Rock 'n' Roll Hall of Fame. We gotta stop there before moving on to L.A., a city synonymous with stardom and a style that says anything goes. The recipes in this chapter are as eclectic as the dive bars, cocktail spots, sideshows, and speakeasies that earned Hollywood its air of glamour, mystery, and longstanding allure. Sip your way through my Cabo Wabo Hollywood favorites like my accelerated Can't Drive 55, legendary Crazy Hagar Cocktail, backstage Southbound Greyhound, tantalizing Strawberry Surf, and stylish Black & Blue Lemonade. No matter what drinks you choose for your next A-list party, once the sun goes down, they'll give you plenty of stories to tell.

Filled with colorful anecdotes and an Encore chapter to give you a taste of even more of my personal favorites, along with a Cocktail Foundations section that reveals the secrets to my homemade purees, syrups, mixers, and salts, this greatest-hits cocktail book will be the definitive guide for drink lovers and backyard bartenders. The same way I make music to share with my fans, I've created these cocktails to share with my friends. When someone comes up and says to me, "Man, that was such a great cocktail. How'd you make that?" it's just as rewarding as hearing, "Man, I love your music—I grew up on your songs." So here are the best of my recipes and a toast to the good life.

I hope you have as much fun drinking these cocktails as I've had making them.

The Home Bar

CREATING THE SPACE

Every time I open a new beach bar or cantina, I think about the way I want people to feel when they visit. The answer to that one question helps me create the right atmosphere—and the right cocktail list to keep it at the forefront.

You'll see that same philosophy reflected in the unique, fun-filled chapters in this book. Each one is a nod to a different lifestyle and includes a can't-miss list of recipes designed to suit the moods I get from places I've lived or love to visit. Think of it like a guided cocktail tour from a chilled-out Hawaiian paradise to a colorful, rowdy cantina, to an after-hours Vegas VIP club, and finally to the movie stars-meet-rock stars glamour of Hollywood's industry parties. If I'm doing my job right, one of these lifestyles will inspire you to set up your own home bar as a celebration of the lifestyle you like best.

As you read, you'll see that every chapter offers specific advice about transforming your space, but there's no one way to do it. Maybe your home bar is a corner in the living room in a one-bedroom apartment. Maybe you're working with a basement cave, a backyard patio, or a poolside sun deck. All are perfect options, so long as you have easy access to your bar tools, liquor, glasses, and fresh ice. Otherwise, you might not make drinks as often as you like. When you're creating a space from a feeling, it can exist in any room of any size, as well as the great outdoors. I've seen home bars put together in different ways— bar carts, cupboards, or milk crate castles. The trick is to design your bar intentionally and stock it with all the flavors that make you feel…well, like a rock star.

Ask yourself: are people coming over to chill out or to party? Do you want them to feel like family or VIP guests? Is music the main event, or part of the background experience? Do you want people to sit at the bar, lounge nearby, or spill out onto the lawn? Just keep in mind that a bar can look incredibly cool, but no one's going back if the drinks don't measure up. That's where I come in.

My goal is to set you up for success across the board with a few bartending basics, tips and tricks, the right equipment, plus a few behind-the-scenes stories to entertain you along the way. There's really only one rule to transforming your space: let your home bar reflect your vacation dreams, personal style, obsessions, or the place that changed your life the way Cabo changed mine. Once that's done, turn all of your attention to mixing the kinds of cocktails that'll transport your guests from the very first sip of their cocktails, expertly crafted by you.

STOCKING THE LIQUOR CABINET

oday, we have access to a huge selection of products from all over the world, most of which are accessible any time of the year. Personally, I like to work with my rum and tequila brands whenever possible. But I also use a wide range of other products from other companies and other countries, so it's important you make your choices based on the quality of the spirit/brand, flavor, and price-point. Ultimately, the better your base spirits and accompanying ingredients are, the better your drinks will be.

In the chapters that follow, I offer some ideas about how to create a custom cocktail list around my lifestyle-inspired drinks; from there, you can expand your liquor cabinet a little at a time, one party at a time. Once your shelves are eventually stocked, you'll be ready for everything, from an intimate happy hour to an enviable theme party, to an all-night bash that only ends when the sun comes up.

In my home, I have both general liquors and liqueurs as well as bottles that are brand-specific, such as Sammy's Beach Bar Rums, Santo Tequilas and Mezquila, and Cabo Wabo Tequilas, which is just my way of telling you what I like best and what I'm most proud of. Substitute your own favorites or try one of my personal recommendations for the most true-to-the-real thing cocktail flavors. Either way, we're all about to have a real good time; it's tough to go wrong when you're making cocktails with friends.

Equipment, Tools & Accessories

You don't need many items to set up your home bar, but you'll run into trouble if you don't have everything you need within reach. Outfit your bar before the party starts, and use this list as a starting point:

BARTENDER'S KNIFE AND CUTTING BOARD
Keep a sharp bartender's knife or paring knife on hand along with a cutting board; a dull knife is more dangerous, and you never know when you'll need to refresh your garnishes. Put a bar towel under your cutting board to keep it from sliding.

BLENDER
You'll need a high quality bar or kitchen blender to make the most of my cocktail list; be sure to buy one that's specifically designed to crush ice. After you're done making cocktails, blend some water with soap to help rinse fruit pulp from the blades.

COASTERS
Avoid rings, especially on your nice furniture, with coasters. I like to collect them from my favorite bars. Try stone, metal, cardboard, useable, recyclable, upcycled, you name it.

CHANNEL KNIFE
You can use a paring knife to cut a citrus twist, but it's trickier and more time consuming. I'd recommend you get a channel knife to easily create a twist.

CITRUS JUICER OR SQUEEZER
If you ask me, juice is a make-or-break ingredient; I always say make it fresh if you can. If you can't, or don't have time, be sure to buy freshly-squeezed. If you plan to throw a lot of big parties, I'd invest in a juicer, so you don't have to spend hours squeezing citrus, or other fruits and veggies, by hand.

COCKTAIL SHAKERS

I like metal shakers myself, rather than a pint glass over a metal cup. Your drinks will get colder faster and there's no broken glass to deal with if you laugh too hard and lose your grip. There's no bigger party foul than a trip to the ER. The Boston Shaker has two stainless steel cups that fit together tight enough to shake without spilling. The Cobbler includes a built in strainer and (often) a lid that doubles as a jigger. Both work just fine; stock your bar with both if you're not sure what you like to work with. One night of making cocktails will make the decision for you.

ICE MOLDS OR TRAYS, BUCKET, AND SCOOP

Bartenders can get pretty serious about their ice: different shapes for different cocktails, perfectly clear cubes or spheres. But I've just got two rules: make sure your water is filtered and your ice is clear and fresh. Ice from your fridge's icemaker is fine; you just don't want it to bring any flavor to your cocktail. When in doubt, buy a bag or two of fresh party ice and keep it in a separate freezer or cooler. You can also get crazy with silicone ice molds if you want to, but it's not necessary for my brand of drinks.

JIGGERS

I like using a double jigger—two ounces on one side and one ounce on the other. But there are no real rules except to make sure the measuring lines are easy to read—even if you're on your second (or third) home-bar margarita. Lots of sets have matching tools that look cool—just make sure they're also functional and sturdy.

MIXING SPOON

A bartender's mixing spoon is very long and features a twisted handle. With the right technique, it helps you stir continuously and smoothly without splashing.

MUDDLER

A muddler is a polished stick that's rounded on the bottom, made for gently breaking down certain ingredients. It's great for extracting oils from herbs like mint or juices from fruits like lime. If you love a mojito, you'll soon become a pro at muddling.

PAPER UMBRELLAS

They're not a necessity, but they are a fun extra touch for an extra taste of the tropics.

PLATES

Outfit your bar with a few small plates. You'll need at least one for sugar and one for salt to make rimming your cocktail glasses fast and easy.

POPSICLE MOLDS & STICKS

Not every cocktail will freeze into popsicles like my Waborita & Wabo Pops (page 118). But do try it whenever you can. Just make sure you stick with the high juice to alcohol ratio (anywhere from 4:1 to 8:1) so your liquor will freeze. Nothing says summer like a frozen cocktail, and popsicles are perfect for the pool; no worries about broken glass or drinks that don't stay cold. Find molds in whatever shape you like best—just don't forget the popsicle sticks if they don't come included.

SKEWERS

My vote is for bamboo skewers; they look nicer than plastic, and they're better for the environment. Be sure they're long enough to load with your garnishes and keep from submerging in your glass.

STRAINERS

If you're not sure which type of strainer you like best, pick up a Julep and a Hawthorne. You won't need a fine mesh strainer for my drinks—a little pulp is part of the experience. The Julep is shaped like a large spoon with holes. You hold it over the shaker while you pour, holding back fruit, excess pulp, and ice. Hawthorne strainers have a coiled spring around the edge to help keep them tightly in place when you pour from the shaker.

STRAWS

I keep a few different types on hand, particularly metal spoon straws and bamboo reusable straws. Both are good for crushed ice drinks or anything else that requires one. Generally, I don't recommend straws unless they're the drinks I've mentioned. Paper straws are fine in a pinch but dissolve quickly if the drink isn't consumed fast enough.

WINE KEY

Find a wine key that's durable, comfortable to hold, opens easily, has a sharp knife and a worm (that's the part that twists in) that's not so wide that it shreds the cork. I wouldn't spend a lot on your wine keys—they tend to disappear. But make sure you get one that's bartender-approved.

GLASSWARE

Most people won't have space in their home bars to stock every type of glassware recommended for the cocktails in this book. When picking and choosing, think about your favorite drinks and your preferred party mood. If your bar is sleek and modern, maybe skip the tiki mugs and hurricanes. If you like cocktails on the rocks rather than blended, skip the margarita glasses in favor of highballs. Then again, if you're a firm believer that more is more, go ahead and shop for everything on this list.

At home, I have an assortment of glassware, and those glasses often lean on the small side (except when I'm making larger cocktails like the Coronarita or Wabo Bowl). I find a smaller glass means a drink made with ice will remain relatively colder for a longer period of time as opposed to a larger glass in which the drink—unless I drink it fast—will get warm. And there's nothing worse than a lukewarm cocktail, especially one that's been diluted with melted ice. To further keep your drinks on the cool side, I recommend for those cocktails that call for shaking with ice that you shake, shake, shake the heck out of your drink before pouring. It's also best to chill your glasses (freezer or fill with ice) beforehand.

CATALINA GLASS
Just one of my cocktails calls for a Catalina glass. They look like a tall, slender, more elegant pint glass. They're very cool but more of a splurge than a necessity if space is limited.

CHAMPAGNE FLUTE
Champagne flutes are elegant, tall, slender glasses with long stems. Classics for ringing in the New Year and celebratory toasts. I'd recommend either flutes or coupes for your bar, whichever shape you like best.

COCKTAIL FISHBOWL
For your guests who are daring enough to indulge in the oversized Wabo Bowl (page 166), you'll need a vessel large enough to serve it. This is one, like tiki mugs and margarita glasses, that isn't defined by a specific shape. Find a bowl that works for you, your friends, your parties, and your style.

COLLINS GLASSES

Collins glasses are tall, slim, cylindrical glasses. They're perfect for cocktails on the rocks and great with straws and umbrellas. Any drink that can go into a Collins glass can also work in a highball if you prefer a shorter, wider shape.

COPPER MUGS

Copper mugs are designed to hold plenty of ice. No one says you need copper mugs for mules, but purists love them. And they sure are good to look at, especially with your feet in the sand and the sun dipping below the horizon.

COUPES

Coupes are the shorter, wider champagne glasses you see in movies from the '20s and '30s. I like them for margs and martinis, too, so I tend to buy them more in various sizes than I would if they were reserved for just champagne. That gives me more versatility in my bar.

EXTRA-LARGE SHOT GLASSES

An extra-large shot glass is about 4 ounces, and I'd definitely recommend you have a set on hand for my Lemon Shots—and those moments when nothing but straight tequila will do. I like having a little extra room in the glass even with a full shot; they're easier to carry and drink from when they're not brimming.

GLASS MUGS

Nothing warms you up on a winter night like a hot cocktail. Glass mugs elevate the experience and keep in line with the look of a bar rather than a diner. Find a mug thick enough to keep your hands warm but not burning.

HIGHBALL GLASSES

A highball glass is a tumbler: taller than an Old Fashioned glass (also called a lowball) but shorter and wider than a Collins or zombie glass. If you prefer tall, slim cocktails switch these out for one of those. Highballs have a wider circumference, though. And that's a detail to keep in mind if you like a salt- or sugar-rimmed drink.

HURRICANE GLASSES

Hurricane glasses are tall and curvy, with a low stem. They're great for blended drinks and extravagant garnishes. Only a handful of my cocktails call for them specifically so you could skip the hurricanes and just use a tall glass if you're streamlining your bar—unless you just can't pass up their hourglass shape.

MARGARITA GLASS

Some say that the margarita glass is a variation on the coupe, and it's easy to see why: curved shape, long stem. There are endless variations on margarita glasses: sizes, weights, designs, and colors, so please have fun with these. Get a couple different sizes, even, to go with your different-sized tequila cravings.

MARTINI GLASSES

You can get classic martini glasses in all sorts of sizes, with stems or without. But if you're keeping your bar on the small side (or like to go against the grain), serve your martinis in coupes instead.

MASON JAR

I love serving cocktails from Mason jars. They're not super expensive, they're easy to replace, they're sturdy and easy to wash, and they're a great way to give your party a laid back, welcoming feel. Use these instead of highball glasses, Collins glasses, copper mugs, tiki mugs, or hurricane glasses; they're the most versatile container on this list.

ROCKS OR OLD FASHIONED GLASSES

Rocks glasses go by different names: whisky tumblers, old fashioned glasses, lowballs. You may not need these if you're well-stocked on highballs and you're trying to keep your glassware collection lean.

SNIFTERS

Snifters are round with short stems, wider at the bottom than the top. You may see them called balloons, cognac glasses, brandy snifters, brandy glasses, or brandy bowls. Again, these aren't a necessity unless you're taken with the shape, but they're a great choice for the Añejo Ritual if you don't have a small white wine glass or champagne flute nearby.

TALL TIKI MUGS

The tall tiki mug comes in literally hundreds of sizes, styles, and colors. If tiki drinks are your bar's signature, why not have several collections of these and serve each signature cocktail in its signature mug? Vintage sets are easy to find and a great way to make your home bar truly unique.

TULIP GLASSES

The tulip is traditionally reserved for serving Belgian ales, but I earmark it for my rum, honey, and champagne Cup of Gold. The glass has a short stem and a round body that looks a little like the flower it's named after. This cocktail also looks gorgeous in a coupe, if you're looking for another option.

ZOMBIE GLASS

A zombie glass is the tallest and slimmest of all the cocktail glasses. It was created to show off its namesake cocktail. A highball or Collins could work just as easily—or you could build your whole bar around this lesser-known glass. Especially if you're into colorful cocktails and bright garnishes.

Bartending Basics & Proper Techniques

I like to say that anyone who likes cocktails can be a good bartender. Maybe that's because I purposely keep my recipes on the simple side. You don't need to know tons of fancy techniques to make a bunch of fancy cocktails; you won't be dealing with whipped egg whites or flaming garnishes in this book. But there are a few things every home bartender should know before jumping in:

MEASURE. Some of you are sitting there thinking *that's pretty obvious* and others are thinking *why bother*. My recipes are pretty simple, but that doesn't mean I don't pay attention to the balance of flavors. Use your jigger, and measure carefully. The payoff in your glass is more than worth the extra effort.

MUDDLE. The first rule of muddling is not to over-muddle. You're looking to press and twist, not mash and rip. Especially if you're dealing with mint; you want to release the oils but not the bitter chlorophyll. Put your ingredients in a pint glass or metal shaker and gently (but firmly) muddle until your ingredients get really fragrant. That means the juice or oils are being released, and that's just what you want. Stop there and keep on building your cocktail.

RIM. Seasoning- and salt-rimmed glasses go hand-in-hand with margaritas. But the recipes that follow call for coconut-, sugar-, cinnamon-, honey-, and graham cracker-rimmed glasses as well. The technique is simple: most often, you'll run a notched piece of juicy citrus all the way around the rim of the glass (that's your "glue"), then tip the glass upside down onto a plate of sugar or salt (or coconut, or cinnamon, or whatever else your recipe calls for). Give your glass a few twists of the wrist and it's just that easy: your glass is rimmed with layers of flavor that add a little something extra to each sip of your cocktail. For those who don't prefer an entire rim of seasoning, you can simply "wet" one section of the glass and dip only that part into the seasoning. There are no hard-and-fast-rules when it comes to seasoning the rim.

ROLL AND THROW. You can shake rather than roll and throw if you want to, but I like using this technique when making Bloody Marys. It's a simple method that transfers the cocktail back and forth from one shaker to the next, allowing the drink to chill in one shaker while the other shaker mixes the cocktail without too much dilution or aeration. You also get a thorough mix without the froth that comes from shaking.

SHAKE. Most cocktails that call for fruit juice are shaken. Which means you'll find your rhythm in no time, working your way through the Cabo Wabo and Sammy's Beach Bar & Grill cocktail experience. It's less about the show than the results, though. You're looking for a little dilution, icy coldness, and a frothy finish. Shake it too long and your cocktail gets watery, shake it too short (or without enthusiasm) and you miss out on the aeration you're after, plus the float of tiny ice crystals that sometimes make their way through the strainer.

STIR. Stirring a cocktail with a bar spoon takes some practice, but it's one of the techniques that immediately makes you look like a pro—and makes your cocktails taste like they're made by a pro. Stir when you want to combine and chill your ingredients without a creating a frothy finish. Stirring also keeps your liquor from getting cloudy and overly diluted: two sure signs of an amateur bartender.

To start, add your liquor to a highball glass or your shaker, then fill it halfway with ice. That way if you run out of an ingredient or get sidetracked halfway through, your cocktail isn't just sitting there melting. Grab your bar spoon, hold it with your thumb, pointer and middle fingers, then run the back of the spoon around the inside of the glass for about 30 seconds, using only your wrist. Watch some online tutorials and practice with ice and water until you feel ready for prime time. Too complicated? Just use a chopstick. Same end result, I swear.

STRAIN. You'll almost always strain shaken cocktails and pour them over fresh ice. This keeps them colder—and stronger—for longer, and gives you the exact right amount of texture—you want a bit of pulp, but not too much. Also, cocktails just look better when served with fresh ice. There are a couple different types of strainers to choose from; both work fine. Just as long as you're holding back the partially melted ice, excess pulp, herbs, or fruit, you'll be good to go.

Now, let's make some cocktails!

Sammy Hagar's Cocktail Hits
THE Set List

SPLASH OF ALOHA

I'VE BEEN AN ASPIRING BEACH BUM SINCE I WAS A KID. Growing up in Fontana, about an hour drive from the California coast, my friends and I would pool our money and get there however we could, as often as we could. There we'd be, swimming in the same water, sharing the same sun, same sand, same view as everyone else. Rich, poor, black, white, left, right, it felt everyone was part of the same world no matter how different our worlds really were. Everyone at the beach felt a little like family, and that feeling never changed—even after I grew up, wrote a lot of songs, played a lot of music, and bought a home in Maui where my family and I had lived on and off for twenty-two years. The only difference is that, living on that tropical island, I finally put a name to that beachside energy I'd always gravitated toward: *Aloha.*

Aloha's not just a way to say hello and goodbye; it's a state of mind. A way of living. A state of soul, really. You take a few ounces of compassion, peace, harmony, and affection. Shake 'em up with mutual respect. Drink in kindness and breathe out love. Add a little Sammy's Beach Bar rum, invite your family and friends to swim and play all day, and man—I don't think life gets better than that.

All twenty of my "Splash of Aloha" cocktails in this chapter are inspired by that chilled-out, shoes-off island lifestyle. The tropical lineup is based on drinks I've concocted with my rum and specials you'll find at Sammy's Beach Bar & Grills in Maui and Honolulu. Every bar recipe is easy to make and even easier to drink. That's because they're designed for the

home bartender. Stock up on rum, fruit, and cocktail umbrellas; queue up a playlist heavy on ukulele and steel guitar, and you're halfway to creating your own beach bar—wherever you live, no matter the season.

Remember, especially all you Redheads out there, aloha's a lifestyle. Tropical cocktails, luaus, and tiki parties aren't just for sunny skies and sugar-white beaches. Hell, who even cares if it's summer? I won't deny the magic of sipping rum drinks all day at a poolside party or kicking back with my feet in the warm sand beneath the shady canopy of a palm, but they taste just as good on a lazy backyard afternoon with the sprinkler on. Or in the dead of winter, as the feel-good antidote to the landlocked gray-day blues. Any space, any time, any place can feel like a beach bar, with just a few key ingredients.

For me, everything starts with music. There's no faster way to transport yourself (or a party) straight to Hawaii than to melt into the iconic sound of ukulele. My collection is heavy on Israel Kamakawiwo'ole, Eddie Kamae and his band Sons of Hawaii; Jesse Kalima, Don Ho, Genoa Keawe, Cliff Edwards—the list goes on. You can mix in pahu drums or nature sounds if that feels good: bird calls, breaking waves. While you're hanging out with your friends, shuffle in some tracks from *Sammy Hagar & Friends* to hear some great duets and familiar voices. Mix in some tunes by me and The Wabos, too; especially the instrumental "Maui Wowie." I'm a big Elvis fan, so the *Blue Hawaii* soundtrack gets a lot of rotation at my Beach Bars. Maybe keep the movie playing in the background, too, if your at-home bar needs a little early-sixties inspiration. You can't have too much Elvis or too many aloha shirts when enjoying the island vibe.

Once your music's all sorted, head over to the hardware store for tiki torches. Parties and beach bars need fire, and torches will add to the mood once the sun goes down. You can also add some bamboo fencing; there's no faster way to transform any space into an island-themed getaway. Just know that while creating an atmosphere is important, nothing matters more than the way you greet your guests.

Present everyone with a lei and, if you're a softie like me, kiss them on the cheek when they arrive. It's the traditional Hawaiian greeting, and the lei is a good-luck symbol of friendship, welcome, and hospitality. These are just two simple ways to practice and share aloha. You can easily find leis made from shells or kukui nuts if fresh flowers aren't an option. My personal advice is not to pass on real hibiscus flowers, if you can find them.

Few things say paradise like bright, tropical hibiscus. The flowers don't have a strong scent and they're also edible, with citrusy, cranberry-ish characteristics. Float them in my Maui Rocker or any of the other drinks ahead, scatter the petals over a salad, or plate them alongside your luau-inspired buffet. I'm not much of a dessert guy, so I keep that part of the menu simple: tropical fruit and a splash of macadamia-infused Red Head Rum on the rocks with a twist.

Which brings us to the heart of the party:

cocktails. If you want to try every "Splash of Aloha" recipe, you'll need three of my Sammy's Beach Bar rums—platinum, Red Head, and Kona Spiced—a bottle of my Santo Blanco Tequila, a supporting cast of seven other liquors, and a bottle of bitters.

Once you've got your spirits on hand, your job is to find the freshest fruit possible. I won't tell you to put on a sarong, take out a machete, and husk your own coconuts, though that's something I do when I can. But I will say that the real taste of the tropics depends on ripe, aromatic fruit; you'll see what I mean, as soon as you start flipping through this chapter.

I've included some familiar Cuban and tiki classics: traditional bursts of pineapple, mango, coconut, and lime. None of that's broken, and I wouldn't try to fix it. But I have put my own spin on some well-known recipes and introduced uniquely Hawaiian flavors to keep the old standards from feeling overplayed.

There's really no way to go wrong with this collection of island-inspired beverages, just as there's no bad way to bring a little Hawaii into your home to share with your family and friends.

Shoes off and bottoms up.

808 MOJITO

Aloha! To many, the mojito represents the quintessential rum cocktail. Not surprising, since this historic drink dates back to sixteenth century Cuba where the indigenous ingredients of rum, lime, mint, and cane sugar derive. Traditionally served over ice in a Collins or highball glass, the mojito can be welcomed any time of year. To add a Hawaiian twist to this Cuban classic, I'm incorporating fresh pineapple and mango, habanero pepper, yuzu, kaffir lime leaves, and fruit from the lychee, a beloved tree here in Hawaii. You can also buy lychee fruit online from retailers like Tropical Fruit Box. Fresh lychee has delicate perfume-floral characteristics with notes of honey and melon and is best when making my homemade Lychee Simple Syrup, used in this recipe. Easy, refreshing, and downright delicious, the 808 Mojito has everything that's symbolic about the famous rum cocktail.

½ ounce fresh pineapple (purée, juice, or freshly chopped)

½ ounce fresh mango (purée, juice, or freshly chopped)

½ habanero pepper, chopped

2 ounces fresh yuzu juice

3–4 fresh kaffir lime leaves

1 ounce Lychee Simple Syrup (page 233)

2 ounces Sammy's Beach Bar Platinum Rum

1 ounce ginger beer

¾ ounce Sammy's Red Head Rum

GARNISH:
Fresh mint sprig

In a cocktail shaker, add the pineapple, mango, habanero pepper, yuzu, lime leaves, and Lychee Simple Syrup. Using a muddler, gently (yet firmly) muddle the ingredients. Then add the Beach Bar Platinum Rum. Stir well and pour into a Collins or highball glass filled with crushed ice. Top with the ginger beer and Red Head Rum. Garnish with a fresh mint spring.

COCONUT MOJITO

A quick, cooling drink is just moments away and, man, do I dig this coconutty cocktail. It's a straightforward recipe and an obvious riff on the classic. It pairs traditional mojito ingredients of rum, lime, mint, and cane sugar with the tropical nuances of coconut. To me, this smooth, creamy drink evokes memories of swaying coconut palms and strums of the ukulele. Speaking of strumming a ukulele, you gotta check out the final track from This is Sammy Hagar: When the Party Started, Volume 1. *It's a hidden instrumental that was never meant to be on the album (appears at the end of "Tropic of Capricorn"). One evening, I decided to sit down with a mic in the backyard and play the ukulele amid the chatter of nature. When you hear the crickets chirping, you'll know you found "Maui Wowie," which I happened to do in one take. Enjoy the island melody while sipping a Coconut Mojito. If that doesn't take you to Hawaii, you're not going.*

6–8 fresh mint leaves

1½ teaspoons brown sugar

½ ounce fresh lime juice

1½ ounces Sammy's Beach Bar Platinum Rum

2 ounces coconut water

1½ ounces Coco Lopez Cream of Coconut

1 ounce soda water

RIM:
Coconut cream and toasted coconut flakes

GARNISH:
Fresh mint sprig

Dip the rim of a rocks glass in some coconut cream then roll the moistened rim in toasted coconut flakes. In the prepared glass, add the mint leaves, brown sugar, and lime juice. Using a muddler, gently (yet firmly) muddle the ingredients. Then fill with ice and add the rum, coconut water, and coconut cream. Stir well and top with soda water. Garnish with a fresh mint sprig.

DA KARI

Named after the African word Dakari, *meaning happiness and joy, this easy cocktail is Hawaii in a glass. A fresh piece of muddled pineapple, cane rum, a squeeze of fresh lime juice, and a splash of simple syrup is all you need to taste the tropics. Without question, pineapple cocktails are among the fruitiest drinks you can make. While the piña colada may reign supreme, pineapple can be used in many equally delicious recipes, including the Da Kari. The best way to enjoy one of these babies is standing waist-deep in the turquoise-hued ocean—even if it's just in your imagination. And while you're drinking one, don't forget to play "All We Need Is An Island," the first song I wrote from my album* Sammy Hagar and Friends. *It's a duet with Heart's Nancy Wilson. She brought so much to this song. It's beautiful, and the perfect complement to this cocktail. Funny sidenote: Initially, I was going to lay down the track with Taylor Swift, but I was worried about our age difference. I thought, "What if someone wants us to do a video? People would wonder, 'Is that her grandpa?' Sure, I'm okay with being a grandpa, but not Taylor Swift's grandpa."*

1 large piece fresh pineapple, rind removed

2 ounces Sammy's Beach Bar Platinum Rum

½ fresh lime, squeezed

1 ounce Simple Syrup (page 233)

RIM:
Lime and cane sugar

GARNISH:
Fresh lime wedge

Run a fresh lime wedge around the rim of a chilled martini glass. Then roll the moistened rim in cane sugar and set the glass aside. In a cocktail shaker, add the pineapple. Using a muddler, gently (yet firmly) muddle the pineapple. Then add the rum, lime juice, and Simple Syrup. Fill the shaker with ice and shake well. Strain into the prepared martini glass. Garnish with a fresh lime wedge.

GINGERBREAD MAN

SERVES
1

While vacationing in Maui following a Van Halen world tour in the mid-nineties, my wife and I fell in love with a clifftop retreat on the north shore with a sweeping view of Waipio Bay. After purchasing the home, I met a mad scientist who was making vodka out of pineapples. He also owned a large sugarcane field. "Hey man, you've got all this sugar," I remember telling him. "Shouldn't you be making rum?" It wasn't long before he had me tasting the most mind-blowing, earth-shaking, rock-your-world rum. Shortly after, Sammy's Beach Bar Rum was born. Make yourself a Gingerbread Man with some of my Maui-born rum and you'll taste the difference while dreaming of warm days on the sun-kissed isle.

1½ ounces Sammy's
Beach Bar Platinum Rum

¼ ounce Sammy's
Red Head Rum

¾ ounce Amaro Averna
(Italian bitter digestif)

¼ ounce Monin
Gingerbread Syrup

¼ ounce fresh lime juice

GARNISH:
Fresh orange wheel

In a cocktail shaker filled with ice, add the rums, Amaro Averna, gingerbread syrup, and lime juice. Shake well and strain into a Collins or highball glass filled with ice. Garnish with a fresh orange wheel. **Note:** Depending on the size of your glass, you may need to double the recipe.

GOLDEN TIKI

Tiki cocktails are a ton of fun and as vintage as the Trans Am, a car I happen to dig and sing about early in my career. Like the cool, 6.6-liter driving machine, tiki drinks and tiki-themed parties still remain popular today. So, what exactly constitutes a tiki drink? To me, it's rum—and lots of it—tropical fruit, spices, and layers of flavor. The Golden Tiki features all of these characteristics. Rum and pineapple are natural companions, offering your taste buds a Hawaiian profile that's very delightful. Behind the duo lurks the bold, spicy taste of cognac, a fabulous third wheel for the combo, while the triple sec and agave add the right amount of sweetness and balance. Beautiful in its simplicity, when you're ready for a little spice in your life, the Golden Tiki should do the trick.

1 piece fresh pineapple, rind removed

1½ ounces Sammy's Beach Bar Platinum Rum

½ ounce Bisquit & Dubouché Cognac

½ ounce triple sec (or any high-quality orange liqueur)

½ ounce agave nectar

GARNISH:
Fresh pineapple wedge

In a cocktail shaker, add the pineapple. Using a muddler, gently (yet firmly) muddle the pineapple. Then add the rum, cognac, triple sec, and agave nectar, and fill with ice. Shake well and strain into a hurricane or tall glass filled with ice. Garnish with a fresh pineapple wedge.

HANA REVIVER

Inspired by the unspoiled beauty of Hana, which dangles from Maui's northeastern tip, the Hana Reviver features a couple interesting ingredients you don't often find in a cocktail. While the cane rum and Honey Syrup complement the passion fruit and maraschino liqueur, the bitters and plum powder really fill this drink with intrigue. The Jamaican Jerk bitters bring the intense tastes of the Caribbean into the glass with warm notes of habanero chili, allspice, nutmeg, cinnamon, and thyme. Meanwhile, the Li Hing Mui Powder, made from dried plums and often reserved for sprinkling on tropical fruits including pineapple and papaya, adds dimension with a sweet and sour component and a hint of salty goodness. When you're craving something exotic and different, whip up the Hana Reviver. It'll transport you to Maui every time you taste it.

2 ounces Sammy's Beach Bar Platinum Rum

1 ounce fresh lemon juice

¾ ounce Honey Syrup (page 233)

10 drops Bitter End Jamaican Jerk Bitters

1 very small pinch Li Hing Mui Powder

½ ounce passion fruit nectar

¼ ounce Luxardo Maraschino Liqueur

2 ounces soda water

GARNISH:
Fresh mint sprig

In a mixing glass filled with ice, add the rum, lemon juice, Honey Syrup, bitters, Li Hing Mui Powder, passion fruit nectar, and maraschino liqueur. Stir well and strain into a Collins or highball glass filled with ice. Garnish with a fresh mint sprig. **Note:** You can mildly blend this cocktail if you prefer a slushy cocktail.

MACADAMIA PIÑA-JITO

The first sip of the Macadamia Piña-Jito will prove how well it works. Think of this cocktail as a piña colada and mojito in the same glass and, man, you'll never forget it. It's also the perfect sipper while listening to "Best of Both Worlds" from Van Halen's 5150. While we flip between rough and smooth takes on the same driving riff, I'm trying to figure out what we're on this planet to accomplish. Ultimately, I declare the only thing to do is stop wondering and just make the best of it. Let's make the best of it by mixing up this rum-drenched masterpiece. If you're wondering where the macadamia is in this drink, it's in the float. During the final process of making my Red Head Rum, macadamia nuts are steeped in rum tanks. This allows the nuts to release their oils. The rum is then finished with an all-natural red coloring agent derived from a blend of fruit and vegetable juices. Before serving this cocktail, don't forget to add the toasted coconut, as it's the finishing touch that sets this drink over the top.

4 fresh mint leaves

½ ounce fresh lime juice

3 ounces Coco Lopez Cream of Coconut

4 fresh pineapple chunks

1 ounce Sammy's Beach Bar Platinum Rum

Soda water, as needed

1 ounce Sammy's Red Head Rum

2 or 3 dashes Peychaud's Bitters

GARNISH:
Toasted coconut, fresh pineapple wedge, maraschino cherry

Add the mint leaves to the bottom of a hurricane glass. Using a muddler, gently (yet firmly) muddle the mint, add the lime juice, and set aside. In a bar or kitchen blender, add a couple handfuls of ice along with the cream of coconut, pineapple chunks, and Beach Bar Platinum Rum. Purée until blended. Pour into the hurricane glass that contains the muddled mint and lime juice and top with soda water. Float the Red Head Rum on top along with two or three dashes of bitters. Garnish with toasted coconut, fresh pineapple wedge, and a maraschino cherry.

MAUI MAMA

If you can't make it to the Aloha State anytime soon, don't worry. Relax with this drink, which is the next best thing. I first featured the Maui Mama in my cookbook Are We Having Fun Yet? *and it remains a hit among friends and family. In fact, the other day I knocked one back while listening to "Father Sun" from my album* Sammy Hagar and Friends. *It's a duet with my son Aaron. I wrote the song while on vacation with my family. Incidentally, I bought a Tahitian ukulele on that trip—a weird instrument, but, man, can they sing the most beautiful music. With a dash of coconut syrup and the tart taste of orange juice paired with cane rum, this cocktail will have you practically smelling the ocean breeze while you're chillin' on the patio or beside the pool. With today's strong rum market, there's no better time to try one.*

1½ ounces Sammy's Beach
Bar Platinum Rum

½ ounce Appleton Estate
dark rum

½ ounce Monin
Coconut Syrup

1 ounce fresh orange juice

2 ounces fresh
pineapple juice

Splash of grenadine

GARNISH:
Fresh lemon wedge

In a cocktail shaker filled with ice, add the rums, coconut syrup, and juices. Shake well and strain into a hurricane or tall glass filled with ice. Add a splash of grenadine and garnish with a fresh lemon wedge.

MAUI MARY

The Bloody Mary has gone tropical with my rendition of the illustrious drink. This is a recipe you'll turn to time and again. To me, the Maui Mary is a cultural blend of mainland and Hawaiian flavors. Yes, the Bloody Mary may have its roots in New York, but the Maui Mary makes its home here in Hawaii thanks in part to my Maui-born cane rum. The rum is smooth and a delicious upgrade that enhances this spicy, peppery beverage. When mixing the Mary, I've learned the proper technique is to use the roll and throw technique described below—a quintessential part of the process to ensure the dilution and chill are just right without aeration. For garnishes, purists insist on the traditional celery stalk, which is how we serve them at Sammy's Beach Bar & Grills, but feel free to get creative with a kabob of your favorites including stuffed olives, cocktail onions, mushrooms, cheese, or whatever makes you happy!

2½ ounces Sammy's Beach Bar Platinum Rum

½ ounce fresh lemon juice

1 squeeze fresh lime juice

5 ounces tomato juice

1 dash Tabasco hot sauce

⅛ teaspoon celery salt

⅛ teaspoon freshly ground black pepper

GARNISH:
Fresh lime wedge and celery stalk

In a cocktail shaker filled with ice, add the rum, juices, Tabasco, celery salt, and pepper. Next, place a strainer, like a Hawthorn strainer, over the top of the shaker and pour/strain immediately into another shaker that's empty (with no strainer). Now pour the contents back into the first shaker through the strainer that has the ice. Now back into the empty shaker. Do this back and forth for about 15 seconds. This is called the roll and throw method; transferring the cocktail back and forth from one shaker to the next allows the drink to chill in one shaker while the other shaker mixes the cocktail without too much dilution or aeration. Now, pour/strain one last time into a Collins or highball glass filled with ice. Garnish with a fresh lime wedge and celery stalk.

MAUI ROCKER

This tropical, red-colored libation—perfect for sailors, swimmers, and salty sea dogs alike—was featured on the The Rachael Ray Show *and can really pack a punch. Emeril Lagasse, who's a close friend of mine and who appeared on the show alongside me, watched as I was making one. After I added a little more rum than the recipe calls for, he peered at the audience and quipped, "It's a good thing Rachael sent her driver." To me, recipes are simply guidelines, and a lot of the time, I prefer to wing it. Mix this one up and you're ready for a summer day at the beach, especially if you pair it with a cool summer tune. For recommendations, check out the Summer Song list from my* Top Rock Countdown *radio show. Tracks include Y&T's "Summertime Girls," "All Summer Long" by Kid Rock, and Van Halen's "Summer Nights."*

1½ ounces Sammy's Beach Bar Platinum Rum

1½ ounces fresh pineapple juice

1 ounce Sweet & Sour Mix (page 235)

½ ounce triple sec (or any high-quality orange liqueur)

¼ ounce grenadine

GARNISH:
Fresh orange and pineapple wedges

In a cocktail shaker filled with ice, add the rum, pineapple juice, Sweet & Sour Mix, triple sec, and grenadine. Shake well and strain into a hurricane or tall glass filled with ice. Garnish with fresh orange and pineapple wedges.

MAUI SPICED BEACH

SERVES
1

Beyond easy, the Maui Spiced Beach is a recipe that's effortless and a perfect choice for happy hours or luaus. It's served tall and requires just three ingredients. To say it's refreshing is an understatement. For this drink I'm using Kola Spiced Rum, which blends white cane rum with various ingredients including the kola nut. The result is a spiced rum unlike any other, with hints of coffee and a light finish of vanilla. One sip of this cocktail and you'll be mixing up a second round before the first is gone.

1½ ounces Sammy's Beach Bar Kola Spiced Rum

4 ounces fresh pineapple juice

3 ounces cranberry juice

GARNISH:
Fresh orange and pineapple wedges

In a cocktail shaker filled with ice, add the rum, pineapple juice, and cranberry juice. Shake well and strain into a Collins or highball glass filled with ice. Garnish with fresh orange and pineapple wedges.

MINT MACADAMIA MULE

SERVES
1

The Moscow Mule was born in the 1940s during the heyday of vodka. My version brings the legendary drink up to date with a true island feel while remaining true to its refreshing roots. Combining muddled mint, lime juice, ginger beer, and two of my Hawaii-born rums to round out the ensemble, the Mint Macadamia Mule is simple and incredibly easy to mix. For the ginger beer, my choice is Fever-Tree, which is clean, crisp, and full-bodied thanks to a blend of three fiery gingers from Nigeria, Cochin, and the Ivory Coast. Sip one of these any day of the year. It's also the perfect accompaniment to my album This is Sammy Hagar: When the Party Started, Volume 1, *especially track 13 "No Worries" in which I sing about fun, having a good time, and lying on the beach drinking—what else, man—rum.*

3 fresh mint leaves

½ ounce fresh lime juice

1½ ounces Sammy's Beach Bar Platinum Rum

2½ ounces ginger beer

½ ounce Sammy's Red Head Rum

GARNISH:
Fresh lime wheel dipped in crushed toasted macadamia (from 2 nuts)

In a rocks glass, add the mint and lime juice. Using a muddler, gently (yet firmly) muddle the mint. Add the Beach Bar Rum and ginger beer. Fill the glass with ice and float the Red Head Rum on top. Garnish with a fresh macadamia nut-crusted lime wheel.

PINEAPPLE PIÑA COLADA

First made in Puerto Rico back in 1952, the celebrated pineapple and coconut cream piña colada is traditionally made with rum. Personally, I prefer to amp up this frothy beverage by substituting tequila, which brings me to a funny story. When I was breaking into the liquor business, not everyone took me seriously. They figured I'm a gringo and a rock star—what could I possibly know about tequila? Many assumed, "He's Sammy Hagar. He'll drink anything." But, actually, I won't. I'm proud to say I have a discerning palate, and that palate prefers a fine tequila when blending and sipping the colada. Try it. The only thing missing will be the sand between your toes.

1½ ounces Santo Blanco Tequila

2 ounces Coco López Piña Colada Mix

1½ ounces fresh pineapple juice

GARNISH:
2 fresh lime wheels and a chunk of fresh pineapple

Fill a bar or kitchen blender with some ice and add the tequila, piña colada mix, and pineapple juice. Blend until smooth and creamy and pour into a coupe or margarita glass. Garnish with fresh lime wheels and a fresh pineapple chunk.

POMEGRANATE MOJITO

SERVES
1

Should you find yourself in the mood for a more memorable mojito, take a crack at this invigorating cocktail, which we serve all day long, as we do many other drinks in this chapter, at Sammy's Beach Bar & Grills. In it, muddled lime, mint, and pomegranate are shaken with rum and topped with soda water for a robust and revitalizing beverage. For the pomegranate, I like to use Monin Pomegranate Syrup because it's all-natural and the tart and sweetness really add that extra punch. With rum being the spirit of summer in every possible way, branch out and savor this concoction. It'll keep summer in your heart, even if you aren't visiting the islands anytime soon.

1 ounce Monin Pomegranate Syrup

3 fresh lime wedges

5 fresh mint leaves

1½ ounces Sammy's Beach Bar Platinum Rum

½ ounce soda water

GARNISH:
Fresh mint sprig and lime wedge

In a cocktail shaker, add the pomegranate syrup, limes, and mint leaves. Using a muddler, gently (yet firmly) muddle the ingredients. Add the rum and fill the shaker with ice. Shake and strain into a rocks glass filled with ice. Top with the soda water and garnish with a fresh mint sprig and lime wedge.

RED HEAD MAI TAI

I just love the ocean; I love my feet in the sand. I'm a beach nut, a sun worshipper. I can't help it. I would rather be at the beach than anywhere else. Man, put me on that beach with a chair and this cocktail—I can't get enough of it. When you're craving something uniquely tropical, take time out and make this mai tai. It comes with a Red Head twist, and it's super easy to assemble. A colorful paper parasol scores extra points. When I was on The Rachael Ray Show, *I poured one of these for her. She took a sip, smiled, and belted out to her audience, "Everyone knows Sammy Hagar rocks, but let me tell you, he knows how to mix, too—a great cocktail that is!" The secret is the Red Head Rum, made by my master distiller. He uses white rum as a base, infuses it with macadamia nuts and the highest-quality red coloring agent made from all-natural fruit and vegetable juices, and end ups with a very exotic-tasting rum. Think cordial, and a perfect topper for this fabulous drink.*

1½ ounces Sammy's Beach Bar Platinum Rum

½ ounce triple sec (or any high-quality orange liqueur)

½ ounce orgeat syrup

1 ounce fresh lime juice

1½ ounces fresh pineapple juice

Drizzle of Sammy's Red Head Rum

GARNISH:
Fresh pineapple wedge, maraschino cherry, fresh mint sprig, paper umbrella

In a cocktail shaker filled with ice, add the Beach Bar Rum, triple sec, orgeat syrup, lime juice, and pineapple juice. Shake well and strain into a rocks or snifter glass filled with ice. Drizzle a little of Sammy's Red Head Rum over the top. Garnish with a fresh pineapple wedge, maraschino cherry, fresh mint sprig, and paper umbrella.

RED HEAD ROAST

If you're looking for a spiked coffee cocktail to wake your senses, this is it. Sip one while jamming to "Red" from my album All Night Long, *which segues into "Rock 'n' Roll Weekend." The Red Head Roast is the result of our bartenders getting together with baristas. Best of all, you don't need to work behind a bar or coffee shop to appreciate this buzzy, caffeinated creation. You can comfortably make these at home when your party or luau needs a quick spark—or the morning, depending on how you roll. While some will use the same cup of Joe to get them going in the a.m., I suggest upgrading to a premium roasted coffee bean from your local café or specialty shop and brewing it in a French press (save the drip machine for your morning routine). This is the difference between a decent drink and a spectacular one. My choice is 100 percent Kona coffee, which I allow to get completely cold before adding it to the Red Head Roast for that Big Island jolt.*

1½ ounces Sammy's Red Head Rum

½ ounce Kahlúa Coffee Liquor

2½ ounces iced coffee

½ ounce Simple Syrup (page 233)

¾ ounce cream

GARNISH:
Freshly grated nutmeg and cinnamon

In a cocktail shaker filled with ice, add the rum, coffee liquor, iced coffee, Simple Syrup, and cream. Shake well and strain into a chilled rocks glass. Garnish with freshly grated nutmeg and cinnamon.

ROCKIN' DAIQUIRI

SERVES 1

I won't say no to any chilled cocktail on a humid day, but if you ask me, the best summer drinks are rum drinks--and I'm not the only one. According to a recent nationwide survey, more than 25 percent of Americans say rum is their go-to spirit when the sun's out. It's not just for sailors and privateers anymore. This Rockin' Daiquiri is in heavy rotation anytime I'm in Hawaii. It's an uncomplicated recipe, and a twist on the granddaddy of rum cocktails. As the party nears, you'll make some fresh lychee juice and a batch of homemade sweet & sour mix. Individual limes are expensive at the grocery store, so buy them in bulk by the bag. This casual cocktail has vibrant color and a fun, fruity taste; you can even make it by the pitcher. Just don't overdo the citrus or your cocktail will drown in a puckering pool of acidity.

1½ ounces Sammy's Beach Bar Platinum Rum

1 ounce Sweet & Sour Mix (page 235)

½ ounce fresh Lychee Juice (page 234)

½ ounce fresh pineapple juice

GARNISH:
Fresh lime wedge and orange peel

In a cocktail shaker filled with ice, add the rum, Sweet & Sour Mix, Lychee Juice, and pineapple juice. Shake well and strain into a chilled rocks glass. Garnish with a fresh lime wedge and orange peel.

SHARK BITE

SERVES
1

I remember celebrating the launch of Sammy's Beach Bar Rum at Cabo Wabo Cantina in Las Vegas. I hosted a private event at the Cantina with friends and family in celebration of my newest endeavor. After strolling through the Cantina, greeting fans, and signing bottles of the inaugural rum, close friend Emeril Lagasse, along with some of our pals and wives, cheered to the evening with shots of rum. We then came together to craft a handful of new rum cocktails, including the Shark Bite, which we savored while nibbling on Ahi tostadas, chicken tostadas, and beef skewers. I'm a big fan of this drink, especially when on vacation and kickin' it poolside with my family. The rum pairs well with the citrus in the drink along with the sweet and spiciness of Southern Comfort, an age-old spirit created by a New Orleans bartender in 1874. Apparently, Janis Joplin made a show of swigging the Comfort day and night. Today, I'm sure she'd love to sink her teeth into a Shark Bite. Here's to you, Janis.

1½ ounces Sammy's Beach Bar Platinum Rum

½ ounce Southern Comfort

½ ounce fresh orange juice

1 ounce Sweet & Sour Mix (page 235)

½ ounce Simple Syrup (page 233)

Lemon-lime soda (7-Up or Sprite), as needed

GARNISH:
Fresh pineapple wedge, maraschino cherry, fresh mint sprig, paper umbrella

In a cocktail shaker filled with ice, add the rum, Southern Comfort, orange juice, Sweet & Sour Mix, and Simple Syrup. Shake well and strain into a Collins or highball glass filled with ice. Top with a splash of lemon-lime soda. Garnish with a fresh pineapple wedge, maraschino cherry, fresh mint sprig, and paper umbrella.

TIKI SWIZZLE

Get ready to be transported to the Hawaiian Islands with this tropical concoction, featuring two of my signature rums and what I consider the holy trinity of juices: lime, pineapple, and orange. To elevate the island experience, I've added some fruity South Seas syrup. More than a thousand different islands make up the South Seas Islands, and they're the inspiration for Monin's South Seas Blend. With notes of ripe mango balanced with guava and a little ginger spice, this all-natural syrup is the perfect match. Now, put it all together and, man, you have an impressive cocktail; one I enjoyed far too much one night in Maui after belting out "Poundcake" and performing with Alice Cooper and Steven Tyler during a New Year's Eve charity concert. That was a really cool gig, especially when Steven performed "Dream On" with local Hawaii ukulele legend Willie K.

1¼ ounces Sammy's Beach Bar Platinum Rum

1 ounce Monin South Seas Blend Syrup

½ ounce fresh lime juice

1 ounce fresh pineapple juice

1 ounce fresh orange juice

3 dashes Peychaud's Bitters

¾ ounce Sammy's Red Head Rum

GARNISH:
Fresh pineapple wedge, orange wheel, and maraschino cherry

In a cocktail shaker filled with ice, add the Beach Bar Platinum Rum, Monin South Seas Blend Syrup, juices, bitters, and the Red Head Rum. Shake well and strain into a hurricane or tall glass filled with ice. Garnish with a fresh pineapple wedge, orange wheel, and maraschino cherry.

WAKE UP "SCREAMING"

I don't know about you, but I'm always looking for creative cocktail ideas. This sugar and spice thirst-quencher is one of my island favorites and is featured on my drink menus at Sammy's Beach Bar & Grills, like many others in this chapter. The Wake Up "Screaming" is exhilarating in its simplicity: mix two of my island rums with some pineapple chipotle syrup and fresh pineapple juice and the result is flavortown on ice. The secret is the thrilling combination of the syrup; the juicy, tropical taste of pineapple paired with a kick of chipotle pepper. Made with pure cane sugar like the rums with no artificial sweeteners, the all-natural syrup enhances mixed or blended drinks including the Wake Up "Screaming" without overpowering or being too sugary.

1½ ounces Sammy's Beach Bar Platinum Rum

½ ounce Sammy's Red Head Rum

1½ ounces Monin Pineapple Chipotle Syrup

3 ounces fresh pineapple juice

GARNISH:
Fresh pineapple cubes

In a cocktail shaker filled with ice, add the rums, pineapple chipotle syrup, and pineapple juice. Shake well and strain into a Catalina glass filled with ice. Garnish with a skewer of fresh pineapple cubes.

Mas Tequila

YOU'VE PROBABLY HEARD ME TALK ABOUT MY LOVE AFFAIR WITH CABO SAN LUCAS, WHICH STARTED IN THE LATE SEVENTIES AND HASN'T LET UP FOR A MINUTE. Back then, Cabo was truly remote. Going there felt like going back in time. It had dirt roads and two or three hotels, none of them with air conditioning, phones, or TVs. Believe it or not, that turned out to be the best vacation I've ever had—because it's the place that changed my life.

I bought my first place in Cabo in the early '80s, and even back then I was thinking how cool it'd be to build a tequila bar. Someplace really casual where I could go after a day at the beach, still in shorts and a T-shirt. Bring all my friends, play guitar, listen to great music, and get a little rowdy drinking the most authentic tequila I could find. And that's exactly what happened. Cabo showed me how I want to live—though I'll admit, it took me a minute to get there.

I used to do a lot of cheap tequila shots with salt and lime, chased with a grimace and a big shiver. But as time went on, I spent more time in Mexico, and started drinking better tequila. I even visited the town of Tequila and got turned on to handmade, barrel-aged sipping tequilas that were amber colored, almost like brandy or bourbon. They were so smooth, with a vanilla-toffee flavor. I didn't even know tequila could taste like that. So, I got curious. And you know what happens when I get an idea in my head.

I built Cabo Wabo and started making my own tequila, and both of them turned out to be everything I'd hoped for. I always say Cabo is a place, but Cabo Wabo is a lifestyle. It's about good food, good music, good friends, and kick-ass South-of-the-Border cocktails, like the ones in this fun, festive chapter. It's a lifestyle you can create any place in the world, any time of year—even if you're a thousand miles from Mexico.

I don't have to tell you how much music matters to me; sometimes I like it loud, sometimes chilled out—but at Cabo Wabo, I like an eclectic playlist that's as spicy as the food and drinks. If you're creating a home bar with a cantina-style feel, take a deep dive into Mexican music. Mexico is a big country with a long, rich history—so it's home to some of the most soulful music I've ever heard. Mix in some Mexican Son music, some cumbia, a few ballads about life, love, heartbreak, and history. Add your favorite feel-good beach tunes and some addictive Caribbean rhythms, and your party's already started. If you want to create the true Cabo Wabo lifestyle, throw a few of my songs on your playlist, too: *Dreams-Cabo, Mexico, The Way We Live, Sailin'* and *Let Me Take You There.*

Then, for the real feel of Mexico, you need to transform your space. Atmosphere is everything—and if you're going for a cantina feel you almost can't go too far with color. Bright marine and sky blue; sunset orange, yellow, and red; palm tree green, and neutrals that echo the colors of sand, sun-dried brick, and stucco. Skip the chili-pepper string lights, sombreros, and ponchos; instead, go for shiny tiles, rustic pottery, woven textiles, and candles in cocktail glasses. It just takes a few simple details to bring cozy, authentic touches to your "I'm on vacation; hell yes, we'll have another round" at-home cantina.

If you do things right, you'll have plenty of empty tequila bottles in no time. Save those. Then, get some dahlias—they're the national flower of Mexico, and you'll be amazed at how great they look in old tequila bottles set on top of your bar, tabletop, or shelves. If you can't find dahlias, any bright flower does the trick. You've gotta have some potted succulents, though; there are more than one hundred species of cactus in Baja, so that's a must for a Cabo Wabo-style cantina.

Now—finally—let's talk booze. The recipes in this book are pretty much guaranteed to bring the party. Whether you're celebrating a Mexican fiesta or just getting a little wild on a Friday night, it's easy to transport the salt, smoke, freshness, and spice of Los Cabos into your home. If you're starting from scratch, just stock your bar with the basics; you can expand as you go. To begin, be sure you've got everything you'll need for my margaritas, palomas, sangria, and the perfect diablo: Either Cabo Wabo Blanco for its fiery, clean, agave-forward flavor, or the smooth, peppery, citrusy taste of Santo Blanco Tequila. You'll also need bold, rich, barrel-aged Cabo Wabo Añejo Tequila and Santo Mezquila, an herbaceous, lightly smoky, tequila-mezcal blend. Once you're set with tequila and mezquila, grab a bottle of Carpano Bianco, a fragrant vermouth that's delicious with grapefruit and

ideal for my signature Paloma. Always have a bottle of triple sec on hand, plus Grand Marnier, Damiana Liqueur, Crème de cassis, grenadine, and a bottle of red wine. Stock up on fresh citrus, cilantro, cucumber, soda water, and organic blossom honey syrup, and you're ready for the grand opening.

With just these handful of bottles, you'll be set to serve guests whose favorite cocktails are a cool, refreshing, slightly herbaceous margarita; a classic marg with a twist rumored to work as an aphrodisiac; a dark, rich, slightly fruity concoction literally named after the devil; a drink-all-day-and-night tequila-based sangria; and the most unique, smoky-citrus cocktail you'll ever taste in your life. A few other fruit juices will add a few more cocktails to your repertoire…and soon your at-home cantina will rival any fiesta Cabo Wabo's ever seen.

Once you taste the adventurous cocktails in the pages ahead, you'll get a flavor of the exciting lifestyle I'm talking about. And you'll understand why I spend a lot of my time in Cabo, when I could live anywhere in the world. That town—and really fine tequila—showed me a dream. Once I caught it, I knew I had to live it. And that's what I've been doing for more than forty years. Here's to creating your own cantina and living the Cabo Wabo dream along with me.

Salud!

BLANCO GIMLET

Bienvenida a México! My Blanco Gimlet is Cabo's answer to the classic gimlet and a tasty party beverage any time of year. That's because of the marriage between the Santo Blanco Tequila and a unique chile poblano liqueur. Yeah, man, they really make such a thing. In 1920s Puebla, the cantinas of the Barrio del Artista bustled with artists and intellectuals who gathered to exchange ideas over original homemade liqueurs known as menjurjes. One especially popular menjurje was handcrafted from the ancho chile. At Mexico's Cabo Wabo, we like to pay homage to those original recipes with authentic Mexican liqueurs steeped in the tradition of Puebla. One sip in, and trust me, you'll be transported to a cozy fiesta in no time.

1½ ounces Santo
Blanco Tequila

½ ounce Ancho Reyes Verde
Chile Poblano Liqueur

1 ounce fresh lime juice

½ ounce Simple Syrup
(page 233)

GARNISH:
Fresh lime wheel and
mint leaf

In a rocks glass filled with ice, add the tequila, chile poblano liqueur, lime juice, and Simple Syrup. Stir and garnish with a fresh lime wheel and mint leaf on a skewer.

COCO LOCO

When tequila and a coconut walk into Cabo Wabo, things get crazy. For all you Redheads—or anyone else out there—looking for a painless twist on the traditional margarita, this recipe is for you. Made with 1800 Coconut—a double-distilled silver tequila infused with natural, ripe coconut—this chic margarita offers a smooth, lightly sweet, tropical taste. The Coco Loco is another one of our flavorful margs you'll find at Cabo Wabo. Sip one while belting out "Mas Tequila" from my Red Voodoo album. I sing about a trip down to Baja California where I'm having a good time while enjoying my favorite Mexican beverage—tequila—which I refer to as my "Vitamin T"!

1½ ounces 1800 Coconut Tequila

½ ounce triple sec (or any high-quality orange liqueur)

1 ounce fresh pineapple juice

3 ounces Sweet & Sour Mix (page 235)

RIM:
Fresh lime and sea salt

GARNISH:
Fresh lime wheel

Run a fresh lime wedge around the rim of a chilled margarita or old fashioned glass. Then roll the moistened rim in sea salt and set the glass aside. In a cocktail shaker filled with ice, add the tequila, triple sec, pineapple juice, and Sweet & Sour Mix. Shake well and strain into the prepared glass. Garnish with a fresh lime wheel.

CORONARITA

When you can't decide between an ice-cold Corona and a margarita, I give you the Coronarita—a fan favorite at Cabo Wabo. This cocktail is the perfect answer to a hot summer day, special celebration, or game day. You can also serve it poolside or at your next backyard barbecue. When it comes to fashioning the Coronarita, any large glass will do, but I like showing off the drink in a margarita glass. To me, this fun cocktail is all about presentation—and what better visual than to have an upside down Corona flowing into your delicious marg? I do find the seven-ounce "mini" Coronarita beer an ideal size as opposed to the larger, twelve-ounce Corona. If you do want to use the regular-sized beer, make sure your glass is spacious enough to hold the bottle, or come up with a creative way to secure the beer so the bottle doesn't tip over your drink. Yes, Corona even makes an ingenious beer clip for this very purpose.

1½ ounces Cabo Wabo Blanco Tequila

½ ounce triple sec (or any high-quality orange liqueur)

5 ounces Sweet & Sour Mix (page 235)

1 Corona beer (7- or 12-ounce bottle)

RIM:
Fresh lime and sea salt

Run a fresh lime wedge around the rim of a chilled margarita glass. Then roll the moistened rim in sea salt and set the glass aside. In a cocktail shaker filled with ice, add the tequila, triple sec, and Sweet & Sour Mix. Shake well and strain into the prepared glass. Carefully add the beer by turning the bottle upside down into the glass and serve.

DESERT PEAR MARGARITA

SERVES
1

You can't mention Cabo and the surrounding landscape without mentioning cactus. For those of you who want to work in a little cactus at your next fiesta, serve up a round of these delicious margs. For all you Redheads who like fun facts, the desert pear is another name for prickly pear, the brightly colored fruit that grows on cactus. They're really not a pear at all but shaped like one. To me, the flavor of this arid fruit reminds me of pear, watermelon, and bubble gum all mixed together. Combine that with the natural neon fuchsia color, and it's the perfect wow-worthy ingredient for cocktails like this tasty special that's served up nightly at the Cabo Wabo Cantinas. For you home bartenders, there's no need to harvest and process your own prickly pear syrup. You can buy it ready-made online or at select grocers. Now all that's left to do is add it and shake it up with some mezcal, triple sec, lime, and Sweet & Sour for a refreshingly smoky-sweet cocktail.

1¼ ounces Mezcal
(or Santo Mezquila)

¼ ounce triple sec (or any
high-quality orange liqueur)

1½ ounces prickly pear syrup

½ ounce fresh lime juice

2 ounces Sweet & Sour Mix
(page 235)

RIM:
Fresh lime and sugar

GARNISH:
Fresh lime wheel

Run a fresh lime wedge around the rim of a chilled margarita glass. Then roll the moistened rim in sugar. Fill the glass with ice and set aside. In a cocktail shaker, add the mezcal, triple sec, prickly pear syrup, lime juice, and Sweet & Sour Mix. Shake well and pour into the prepared glass. Garnish with a fresh lime wheel and serve.

EL DIABLO

I'll admit, when I'm here in Mexico, I'm swigging tequila, mezquila, and South-of-the-Border favorites like this one. Listed as one of our signature drinks on the Cabo Wabo menu, the El Diablo is an exciting addition to expand your bartending repertoire. Whether you want to mix it for a future get-together or make one now while rocking out to "Cabo Wabo"—a seven-minute lick about getting drunk on a Mexican beach from Van Halen's OU812—try it with Cabo Wabo Añejo. The tequila's amber color invites you in. A whiff of vanilla raises an eyebrow. Hints of honey wake up your taste buds. With age comes wisdom—and more rich taste—and this aged tequila is the ticket. As most Redheads know, I created Cabo Wabo Tequila. After devoting myself to developing a tequila that embodied my beliefs of living free, working hard, and playing harder, I had some made by a family in Mexico who'd been crafting tequila for generations. Eventually Cabo Wabo Tequila was exported to the United States, where it quickly became a popular premium brand. Try it. I think you'll like it.

1 fresh lemon wedge

¼ ounce Crème de cassis liqueur

1½ ounces Cabo Wabo Añejo Tequila

½ ounce fresh orange juice

Lemon-lime soda (7-Up), as needed

Splash of grenadine

GARNISH:
Fresh lemon wedge

In a rocks glass filled with ice, squeeze the juice of the lemon wedge into the drink. Then add the Crème de cassis, tequila, and orange juice. Stir and top with the lemon-lime soda. Add a splash of grenadine and garnish with a fresh lemon wedge.

GUAVA MARTINI

Cocktail hour will be something memorable with this swanky drink. That's because I'm adding guava and pineapple, which pairs exceptionally well with a top-shelf tequila like Santo Blanco Tequila. Quick story: when Guy Fieri, who's a big tequila lover and dear friend of mine, approached me about creating a tequila together, I remember the timing being perfect. A few months after we shook hands, we were sipping the most amazing blanco tequila we'd ever tasted. For those of you who want a taste of Mexico at home, try this tropical-inspired drink crafted with Santo Blanco Tequila. It's an "old world"-style tequila made with 100 percent Blue Weber Agave from the famed Jalisco Highlands of Mexico. For the guava juice, try to use pink guava to ensure your martini has a lovely rosy glow. Fresh is best when it comes to extracting juice, but brands like Maaza are a good substitute and contain the pink guava we're after.

1½ ounces Santo Blanco Tequila

1 ounce fresh pineapple juice

1 ounce guava juice

GARNISH:
Fresh lime wheel dusted in Tajín

In a cocktail shaker, fill with ice and add the tequila, pineapple juice, and guava juice. Shake well and strain into a chilled martini or coupe glass. Garnish with a fresh lime wheel dusted in Tajín.

JALAPEÑO CABO KISS

This kiss is twice the spice and just as nice. Another one of our Cabo Wabo signature margaritas, I adore the embrace of Cabo Wabo Tequila with a kiss of fresh jalapeño, a smooch of fresh ginger, and the cool peck of fresh, crisp cucumber—all balanced by a subtle touch of triple sec and Sweet & Sour. The rim dusted in Tajín—a Mexican blend of mild chili peppers, lime, and sea salt—makes this cocktail even more inviting. Heck, it makes me want to break out "Three Lock Box." Sorry, Redheads, this tune isn't in reference to a woman's anatomy like some of you might think. It's actually about achieving a combination of mental, physical, and spiritual balance. That's right, this Bay Area dude is somewhat of a peace loving hippie, and that's exactly my state of mind every time I find myself kickin' back in Cabo with this luscious drink pressed against my lips.

1 slice fresh jalapeño

1 slice fresh ginger

1 slice fresh cucumber

1½ ounces Cabo Wabo Blanco Tequila

½ ounce triple sec (or any high-quality orange liqueur)

4 ounces Sweet & Sour Mix (page 235)

RIM:
Fresh lime and Tajín

GARNISH:
Fresh lime wheel

Run a fresh lime wedge around the rim of a rocks or old fashioned glass. Then roll the moistened rim in Tajín and set the glass aside. In a cocktail shaker, add the jalapeño, ginger, and cucumber. Using a muddler, gently (yet firmly) muddle the ingredients. Add the tequila, triple sec, and Sweet & Sour Mix. Fill the shaker with ice and shake. Pour the entire contents into the prepared glass and garnish with a fresh lime wheel.

MANGO PEÑO

Look no further if you prefer your margaritas sweet and spicy. This one might even become one of your new Mexican favorites. For me, when it comes to peppery margaritas, I say the spicier, the better—and this cocktail gets a surefire hit from the freshly muddled jalapeño. Similar in appearance to the Jalapeño Cabo Kiss, Cabo Wabo's signature Mango Peño introduces Cabo Wabo Blanco Tequila alongside triple sec and Sweet & Sour, but with an added splash of my fresh Mango Purée. I find the Mango Peño has just the right amount of sweet, smoky, and salty to accentuate the heat, making this a gratifying cocktail, especially when grilling outside. In fact, on my last trip to Mexico, I'm pretty sure I drank my weight in Mango Peños.

2 slices fresh jalapeño

1½ ounces Cabo Wabo Blanco Tequila

½ ounce triple sec (or any high-quality orange liqueur)

1 ounce Mango Purée (page 232)

3 ounces Sweet & Sour Mix (page 235)

RIM:
Fresh lime and Tajín

GARNISH:
Fresh lime wheel

Run a fresh lime wedge around the rim of a rocks or old fashioned glass. Then roll the moistened rim in Tajín and set the glass aside. In a cocktail shaker, add the jalapeño slices. Using a muddler, gently (yet firmly) muddle the jalapeño. Add the tequila, triple sec, Mango Purée, and Sweet & Sour Mix. Fill the shaker with ice and shake. Pour the entire contents into the prepared glass and garnish with a fresh lime wheel.

MARGARITA VERDE

Sure, mastering the margarita requires a certain amount of practice, but once you get it dialed in, it's a straightforward cocktail to make. This margarita adventure—served daily at Cabo Wabo—begins with two prominent ingredients used in Mexican cuisine: cucumber and cilantro. The cool muddled cucumber and cilantro balance the bite of the tequila. Then I like to shake up the margarita game by bringing out some of that orange cognac–flavored Grand Marnier to really get things rolling with the tequila, lime juice, and homemade Sweet & Sour Mix. To save pre-party prep time in your cocina, make the mix ahead of time. Also, keep in mind, unlike the reliable lemon, the flavor of limes can vary considerably depending on variety, season, weather, and origin. I always taste my limes first before adding their juice to my drinks. That way, should I have an aggressively sour lime, I can use less than what the recipe calls for.

1 tablespoon peeled and diced fresh cucumber

1 teaspoon fresh chopped cilantro (leaves only)

1½ ounces Cabo Wabo Blanco Tequila

¼ ounce Grand Marnier

½ ounce fresh lime juice

4 ounces Sweet & Sour Mix (page 235)

In a cocktail shaker, add the cucumber and cilantro. Using a muddler, gently (yet firmly) muddle the ingredients. Add the tequila, Grand Marnier, lime juice, and Sweet & Sour Mix. Fill the shaker with ice and shake. Pour the entire contents into a rocks or margarita glass and serve.

SAMMY'S "VELVET KICKSTAND" MARGARITA

Despite the ongoing debate over who served the first margarita—I hear it was some cantina in Ensenada, Rosarito, or Tijuana—this celebrated cocktail is still sought-after one hundred years later. As purists know, the marg's foundation is tequila, orange liqueur or simple syrup, and lime juice. Of course, there are countless variations today. That means, ultimately, there's really no wrong way to make one. And I like that, because I'm not about perfection. I'm about realness and what tastes enjoyable to me. My margarita highlights tequila, orange liqueur, and lime juice and also welcomes a burst of Damiana, a light herbal-based liqueur from Mexico. Damiana derives from the damiana herb—an aphrodisiac—that grows wild in Baja. The bottle is uniquely shaped and modeled after an Incan Goddess. The drink's nickname "Velvet Kickstand" is my play on this liqueur. For the salted rim, I like making my own sea salt (page 235) when I'm down here in Cabo. I make it exclusively for my margaritas. Damn, it's some salty salt! A little goes a long way, and it's flakey enough to disappear on the tongue.

2 ounces Santo
Blanco Tequila

½ ounce triple sec (or any
high-quality orange liqueur)

1 ounce fresh lime juice

½ ounce Damiana Liqueur

RIM:
Fresh lime and
Sammy's Sea Salt
(page 235)

Run a fresh lime wedge around the rim of a chilled margarita or martini glass. Then roll the moistened rim in Sammy's Sea Salt and set the glass aside. In a cocktail shaker filled with ice, add the tequila, triple sec, lime juice, and Damiana Liqueur. Shake well and strain into the prepared glass and serve.

SAMMY'S SANGRIA

SERVES
1

Somewhere between a fruit punch and goblet of wine lives the sangria. For any of you Redheads who are history buffs, you'll be interested to know that more than two thousand years ago, the Romans used to fortify their wine with herbs and spices. The earliest versions of what we now know as sangria were made in England and France in the 1800s. After its formal arrival in the United States at the 1964 World's Fair in New York, the sangria became popularized. Today, this sweet, luscious concoction—traditionally served by the glass or by the pitcher—is a front-runner of mine during summer as tempting foods, family gossip, and music are shared on my back deck. It's also a foolproof drink to rock out to "Bad Motor Scooter"—the first ballad I ever wrote in my life while with Montrose. What makes my Sangria so quintessentially Mexican is the use of tequila that acts as a bold companion to the wine. Believe me, I've tasted, tested, researched, retested, and what I've come up with is this five-ingredient, hot-weather sangria that has everything I'm looking for—it's smooth, refreshing, and boozy. This recipe is my humble offering to the sangria-loving world.

1½ ounces Santo
Blanco Tequila

4 ounces fresh orange juice

½ ounce fresh lime juice

Splash of red wine

Splash of mineral water

GARNISH:
Fresh orange wheel and
maraschino cherry

In a Mason jar filled with ice, add the tequila, orange juice, and lime juice, and stir. Top with a splash of red wine and mineral water, and garnish with a fresh orange wheel and maraschino cherry.

SANTORITA

Like anything to do with food or beverages, I'm a firm believer that the fresher the ingredients, the better the ingredients, and in this case, the better the cocktail. For my Santorita, that begins with raw citrus. The juice of a ripe orange brings out the smokiness of the agave while the tartness of fresh lime balances the drink's sweetness. If you like, you can tweak the measurements of agave nectar and triple sec. For example, if you prefer the taste of agave and want to use more of it, go for it. Just use less triple sec, and vice versa. Otherwise, your cocktail will be too syrupy on the palate. By the way, I never drink during the day—never have—unless I'm on vacation. Should I find myself chillin' in Mexico and crave a Santorita around lunchtime, I'll make this treasured cocktail with rum. But, once the sun goes down, you'll find me knocking these back with mezquila.

1 ounce fresh lime juice

1 ounce fresh orange juice

¼ teaspoon agave nectar

1 ounce triple sec (or any high-quality orange liqueur)

1½ ounce Santo Mezquila (or Sammy's Beach Bar Platinum Rum)

RIM:
Fresh lime and sea salt

Run a fresh lime wedge around the rim of a chilled margarita or martini glass. Then roll the moistened rim in sea salt and set the glass aside. In a cocktail shaker filled with ice, add the lime juice, orange juice, agave nectar, triple sec, and mezquila (or rum). Shake well and strain into the prepared glass and serve.

SANTO BANDIDO

Another signature drink I dig on the Cabo Wabo menu is the Santo Bandido. Whether you're itching for a drink to cushion the blow of missing out on a trip to the pulsating party capital of Cabo, or simply longing for smoky flavors relished on your last trip to the "End of the Earth," pull out a Mason jar and whip up one of these bad boys. The Bandido features a lively, relatively mild melon-flavored liqueur that's seldom used these days. Because Midori makes beautiful drinks— thanks to its electric green color—I find it a very appealing liqueur and one you should keep on hand in your home bar. The melon flavor—recognizable but not overpowering—partners well with the acidity of the lime and pineapple juices of the Bandido, offering you and your guests a smooth and friendly punch to your tastebuds. Mix one up while banging your head to "There's Only One Way to Rock." As you know, this track's been played at nearly every Sammy-fronted Van Halen concert—where the great Eddie Van Halen and I would duel it out on stage with our guitars.

1½ ounces Santo Mezquila

½ ounce Simple Syrup (page 233)

½ ounce fresh lime juice

½ ounce Midori Melon Liqueur

Splash of fresh pineapple juice

RIM:
Fresh lime and Chipotle Sea Salt (page 235)

GARNISH:
Fresh pineapple wedge, cucumber wheel, maraschino cherry

Run a fresh lime wedge around the rim of a Mason jar. Then roll the moistened rim in Chipotle Sea Salt. Fill the prepared jar with ice, add the mezquila, Simple Syrup, lime juice, melon liqueur, and stir. Top with a splash of pineapple juice, and garnish with a fresh pineapple wedge, cucumber wheel, and maraschino cherry on a skewer.

SANTO OAXACA

If you're ready for an intoxicating rum cocktail with the smoky qualities of an Oaxaca-inspired mezcal, you gotta try this one. Yeah, I agree. On paper, the Santo Oaxaca is one hot mess. Mezquila, three rums—one of them overproof—a sweet-tart liquor, and absinthe slugging it out in a single glass, along with lime and pineapple juice, cinnamon syrup, and some double strength hibiscus tea. The recipe reads more like a red-flag ratio rife with morning-after consequences. And yet, somehow it works. The Santo Oaxaca is precisely what I need every now and then, and that's why I love this drink for what it is—an easy swigging, one-and-done stiffy. Unfortunately, they no longer make Bacardi 151—the fiery stuff we all chugged after our girlfriends left us "High and Dry Again,"—but there are other overproof rums available on the market today, like Plantation or Pusser's British Navy.

2 ounces Santo Mezquila

2 ounces overproof rum

1 ounce Zaya rum

1 ounce Sammy's Beach Bar Platinum Rum

1 ounce Velvet Falernum

1 ounce fresh lime juice

½ ounce fresh pineapple juice

½ ounce cinnamon syrup

½ ounce hibiscus tea (double strength)

1 splash absinthe

GARNISH:
Fresh citrus peel, mint sprig, lime wheel, dried hibiscus flower

In a cocktail shaker filled with ice, add the Santo Mezquila, rums, Velvet Falernum, lime juice, pineapple juice, cinnamon syrup, hibiscus tea, and absinthe. Shake well and strain into a zombie glass or tall tiki mug filled with crushed ice. Garnish with a fresh citrus peel, mint sprig, lime wheel, and dried hibiscus flower.

SANTO PALOMA

The Paloma—considered a working man's drink, consisting of just tequila, grapefruit soda, and lime—gets a makeover at Cabo Wabo. At our Cantina, you can spot Mexican locals, American tourists, and me with this cocktail in hand (not to be confused with the Santo Oaxaca, which looks strikingly similar). This twist on one of Mexico's most celebrated drinks is loaded with flavor thanks to the addition of the smoky and herbaceous mezquila, blossom honey syrup, and Carpano Bianco's dry vermouth. Instead of grapefruit soda, I add fresh ruby red grapefruit juice and lime juice, a pinch of salt, and a float of Topo Chico, a sparkling mineral water from Mexico. The Santo Paloma is super-refreshing and as genuinely Mexican as it gets, especially amid Cabo's 340-plus days of sunshine and cooling sea breezes. Enjoy one while we break out the piano for that make-the-most-of-each-day anthem "Right Now"—a special song that happens to mean a lot to Michael Anthony and me, and one that we played with The Circle as a tribute to Eddie Van Halen right after his passing.

1½ ounce Santo Mezquila

½ ounce organic blossom honey syrup

1½ ounces Carpano Bianco

1 ounce fresh ruby red grapefruit juice

½ ounce fresh lime juice

Pinch of salt

1½ ounces Topo Chico mineral water

GARNISH:
Fresh grapefruit wheel and ginger slice

In a cocktail shaker filled with ice, add the mezquila, organic blossom honey syrup, Carpano Bianco, grapefruit juice, lime juice, and salt. Shake well and strain into a rocks glass filled with ice. Top with the Topo Chico and garnish with a fresh grapefruit wheel and slice of ginger.

SANTO SUNRISE

Orange, grenadine, and Blue Curaçao give this jewel of a cocktail—a riff on the classic Tequila Sunrise—its emerald-green color. Mezquila offers the kick. Switching out the typical booze might seem like a minor tweak, but the smoky mezquila is el corazón *(the heart) of this drink's bolder bite. There's enough juice to temper the alcohol content, so you can go round after round with a cocktail more daring than a Screwdriver, and more distinctive than a typical Sunrise. This one goes down real easy—a lot like "Down the Drain," a song my band Chickenfoot and I wrote live in the studio and recorded in one take.*

1½ ounces Santo Mezquila
4 ounces fresh orange juice
Splash of Blue Curaçao
Splash of grenadine

GARNISH:
Fresh halved orange wheel

In a tall glass filled with ice, add the mezquila, orange juice, Blue Curaçao, and grenadine. Garnish with a fresh halved orange wheel.

THE EL SANTO

You may find a number of cocktail recipes out there all named El Santo, but you should commit this one to memory. It's a party-in-your-mouth mix of mezquila, pineapple and orange juice, agave, and a kick of jalapeño and chipotle for that extra zing. This is another welcomed drink at Cabo Wabo, and it's perfect if you're after a Mexican sipper that isn't a margarita. For you mezcal connoisseurs, you'll flip over the Santo Mezquila, the world's first agave blend made from 100 percent Blue Weber Agave and 100 percent Espadin Agave. The outcome is a taste revelation that offers a unique smokiness to the cocktail's blend of sweet heat and fruit flavor. Warning: These go down surprisingly easy. Just having one feels like a mini-vacation down south—and that's often what I need. I've been working my whole life and have always been so damn busy. When I crave some serious downtime, you'll often find me on the sandy shores of Cabo with one of these in hand—admiring the humpbacks behind El Arco, the iconic arch where the Sea of Cortez meets the blue Pacific.

2 slices fresh
jalapeño pepper

1 dash Chipotle Sea Salt
(page 235)

1¼ ounces Santo Mezquila

2 ounces fresh
pineapple juice

Splash fresh orange juice

¼ ounce agave nectar

RIM:
Fresh lime and
Chipotle Sea Salt
(page 235)

Run a fresh lime wedge around the rim of a rocks glass. Then roll the moistened rim in Chipotle Sea Salt and set the glass aside. In a cocktail shaker, add the jalapeño slices and the dash of Chipotle Sea Salt. Using a muddler, gently (yet firmly) muddle the ingredients. Add the mezquila, pineapple and orange juices, and agave nectar. Fill the shaker with ice and shake. Pour the entire contents into the prepared glass and serve.

VINNIE PAUL

This tempting beverage pays tribute to the late Vinnie Paul, Pantera's earth-riffing drummer and a good friend of mine who passed away at the young age of fifty-four. From the beginning, Vinnie had been at nearly every birthday bash of mine at Cabo Wabo. I remember being at the Cantina when I received the news of his loss. It was hard to believe he was gone. He was a drumming pioneer, a great dude, and a dear friend. Naturally, I had to make a drink in his honor. Mix one up while appreciating Vinnie's sliding groves from "Mouth of War." His drums mimic the guitar in perfect harmony—just like this cocktail. At first sip, lime and grapefruit refresh the taste buds, but soon the spicy undertones of Blue Weber Agave from the tequila creep over the palate. A touch of Ancho Chile adds the final veil of mystery.

1½ ounces Santo Blanco Tequila

1 ounce Ancho Reyes Ancho Chile Liqueur

1 ounce fresh lime juice

4 ounces fresh grapefruit juice

½ ounce Simple Syrup (page 233)

GARNISH:
Fresh quartered grapefruit wheel

In a Collins or highball glass filled with ice, add the tequila, chile liqueur, lime juice, grapefruit juice, and Simple Syrup. Stir well and garnish with a fresh quartered grapefruit wheel.

WABORITA & WABO POP

If you've spent any time at Mexico's Cabo Wabo, you've no doubt been served a Waborita—a splashy tequila concoction that is as vibrant as the Cantina itself. This flavor-packed sipper is a fixture at Cabo Wabo and another one of my personal recommendations. Aged reposado tequila adds smooth vanilla notes to a light, citrusy twist on the classic margarita. For a curveball, I like to float a Wabo Pop inside the drink, which is how we serve this Mexican-inspired libation to our thirsty fans down here needing a break from the sun. Keep in mind, at Cabo Wabo we have high temperature industrial-grade freezers that can solidify liquor. Your icebox in the kitchen won't be able to achieve this so you'll need to modify the recipe if you want to freeze and float the popsicle at home, which I explain below. Indulge in a Wabo Pop while tripping out to the effects and spacey middle interlude of Montrose's "Space Station #5." You'll dig it.

1 ounce Cabo Wabo
Reposado Tequila

½ ounce Damiana Liqueur

½ ounce triple sec (or any
high-quality orange liqueur)

½ ounce fresh lime juice

Splash of Blue Curaçao

RIM:
Fresh lime and sea salt

GARNISH:
Fresh lemon peel

Run a fresh lime wedge around the rim of a chilled martini glass. Then roll the moistened rim in sea salt and set the glass aside. In a cocktail shaker filled with ice, add the tequila, Damiana Liqueur, triple sec, and lime juice. Shake and strain into the prepared glass. Add a splash of Blue Curaçao and garnish with a fresh lemon peel.

If you want to turn your Waborita into a Wabo Pop, combine 7 ounces Sweet & Sour Mix (page 235), 1 ounce fresh lime juice, ½ ounce tequila, and a splash of Blue Curaçao to a mixing glass. This will achieve the higher juice to alcohol ratio so you can freeze at home. Now stir well and pour the mixture into molds, complete with a stick (or handle) and place in the freezer. Depending on the size of your molds, this should make 6 pops. When frozen solid, remove and float the popsicle inside a freshly made Waborita.

WATERMELON CUCUMBER FRESCA

Several years ago, on a scorching, arid day in Baja, I met a farmer who was making margaritas from the watermelon and cucumber growing on his ranch. I happened to be touring his agave fields and remember him handing me this summer drink in a cold Mason jar and saying, "Try this, Sam." Funny, the only person who ever called me Sam was John Cougar Mellencamp. I fell in love immediately with the drink, drank an embarrassing amount of them over the course of my visit, and bamboozled the farmer's sister into sharing the recipe. Today, this ultimate refresher, which I've enhanced by adding mezquila, is a go-to of mine while hanging out in my backyard. I'll even raid my wife's garden to pluck some crisp, off-the-vine cucumber. I tell ya, there's no better way to cool down on a hot leisurely day than to sip one of these. All you need is five simple ingredients, a shaker, and some ice. It's reassuring to know that at any given moment, when I'm not in Mexico, I'm still minutes away from an exhilarating fresca.

2 cubes ripe watermelon

4 pieces fresh cucumber (peeled, quartered, and cut into 4⅛-inch slices)

1 ounce fresh lime juice

2 ounces Santa Blanco Tequila

1 ounce agave nectar

GARNISH:
Fresh watermelon wedge and cucumber wheel

In a cocktail shaker, add the watermelon cubes, cucumber slices, and lime juice. Using a muddler, gently (yet firmly) muddle the ingredients. Fill the shaker with ice and add the tequila and agave nectar. Shake and strain into a Collins glass or Mason jar filled with ice. Garnish with a fresh watermelon wedge and cucumber wheel.

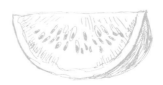

SINFUL SIGNATURES

NOW THAT YOU'VE SPENT SOME TIME WITH ME ENJOYING THE SPIRIT OF ALOHA IN HAWAII AND LIVING IT UP DOWN IN CABO, IT'S TIME TO HIT VEGAS. At the airport, stop into Sammy's Beach Bar & Grill for your kickoff cocktail, then head straight to Cabo Wabo Cantina in the heart of the can't-stop-won't-stop Las Vegas Strip. Go for the live music, neon lights, fast money, risky bets, and celebrity sightings; stay for round after round of the mind-blowing drinks that inspired this chapter's recipes.

Basically, there's only one rule with my Sin City cocktails, even if you're making them at home: have so much fun you can't see straight. Party 'til you need a vacation from your vacation. Keep going 'til you're half dead from feeling so alive. It's been that way in Vegas since the 1930s, when casino gambling and quickie divorces were both legalized. Suddenly the hottest stars, most famous musicians, and sports heroes started flocking to the party capital of the world.

I don't live in Las Vegas full time because I can't keep up the pace. But it's my favorite spot for a few days of live shows, velvet ropes, after-hours parties, and VIP treatment. There are perks to fame, I won't deny it. So, this chapter's about giving you a taste of what it's like to live like a rock star—starting with these cocktails, perfectly paired with the city's trademark blend of glamour and hedonism.

Get ready to pour luxury over excess and garnish it with spectacle. That's the Las Vegas lifestyle, and my sinful cocktails follow suit.

But first, you have to create the right atmosphere. Transforming your home bar into a first-class VIP lounge is simple if you think of it as a feast for all five senses; an after-hours venue fit for superstars and heavyweight champs, where anything you've ever wanted could be yours with one roll of the dice.

Double down on modern shapes and clean lines. Add some low tables and stick to a monochromatic color scheme. Keep things minimal and bet heavy on lighting. Blue or violet bulbs create an other-worldly, mysterious vibe. An orange or yellow glow will amp up the energy. I don't need to tell you that pink and red are just plain sexy. Think about LED light boxes and glass-backed shelves to showcase your top-shelf bottles and glassware.

To get the right feel for your lounge, go big on texture. Hang velvet curtains for an entryway that says you're definitely not in Kansas anymore. Throw down a zebra print rug, even if your lounge is outside.

As for music, anything goes. Make your lounge an EDM lounge, a Motown lounge, or an all-Elvis club with a white-jumpsuit dress code. Whatever you want, Vegas delivers. But it doesn't take a genius to know that my kind of bar is a rock 'n' roll bar. If I'm the DJ, I'm queuing up songs by bands I love and people I know: The Rolling Stones, AC/DC, Aerosmith, Bruce Springsteen, Led Zeppelin, Mötley Crüe, Heart, Alice Cooper, Alice in Chains. I'll mix it up with The Beatles and The Grateful Dead, The Black Keys, whoever else I'm into. You won't be surprised to hear a little Montrose, Van Halen, and Chickenfoot on my playlist.

Now that you're all set with the look, sound, and feel for your VIP lounge, it's time to talk champagne and cocktails. Your only job is to treat your guests like celebrities and high rollers. That means creating a few signature cocktails, drinks they can't get anywhere else. Every party needs its own cocktail menu, catered to the tastes of your VIPs. Good thing you've already got a well-stocked bar. Thanks to my shameless promotion, you may have already picked up Sammy's Beach Bar and Red Head Rums to create your *Splash of Aloha* cocktails, and Santo Blanco Tequila and Mezquila for your *Mas Tequila* drinks (what can I say, I really think they're the best). If so, you're already more than halfway there.

To get a head start on the Sinful Signatures featured in the pages ahead, all you need is some chilled champagne. Start with a toast; that gives you time to mix up a round of Cups of Gold, plus a reason to finish off the bottle of bubbly. In this cocktail, rum, honey, and champagne combine like nectar of the gods. Stay in that lane all night if you want to keep things simple. You'll have a party raging until brunch the next day. Which brings us to morning-after drinks.

Keep the rum rolling with my take on a Kir Royale—infused with macadamia instead of cassis. Or blend up a batch of tequila-laced bellinis; fresh peach staves off the hangover for a few hours longer. Add a float of champagne if you've got any left—the recipe doesn't call for it, but there's no better garnish.

If your day starts with brunch and blended bellinis, don't be surprised if suddenly it's 3 a.m. and you're all still dancing. For VIPs who drink tequila or mezcal, all you need is one more liqueur, three or four syrups, and a few odds and ends from the store before you're set and ready. Make Blood Orange Margaritas, Tamarind Margaritas, and tart, spicy Santo Revelations. One night of taste testing and you'll have your signature cocktails on lockdown—and a line out the door. With each party, add a couple more drinks to your repertoire and soon you'll be making every Sinful Signature—from the cachaça-based Brazilian Kiss to the Key Lime Martini that's better than any pie you've tried.

Even if you don't go so far as to create your own VIP lounge, these are the go-to drinks anytime you and your friends are in the Vegas mindset. When more is more, you've just won big, and you don't care about the hangover, you only need one cocktail: my forty-ounce Wabo Bowl—a boozy concoction that packs one hell of a punch. It's the kind of drink that starts the party and just might end in a two-day bender. Don't say I didn't warn you.

Next time you find yourself on the Las Vegas strip, stop in for a taste of the real thing. We'll see if your Sinful Signatures rival mine. Here's to live shows, late nights, and neon lights. Good friends, even better drinks, and parties that live in infamy.

Let's raise a glass together.

BLOOD ORANGE MARGARITA

Welcome to Vegas, Redheads! You're now a VIP, and it's time you feel like a celebrity and get treated like royalty. Once the sun drops, separate yourself from those trafficking the nightclub scene and fighting for the bartender's attention. You're in the comfort of your own home. That means it's time to grab the shaker behind your bar and kick off the night by mixing up some of my signature Vegas-style cocktails for you and your guests. Remember, every private table is yours when entertaining at your place—even your moonlit patio outside. Best of all, you can come and go as you please. So, let's get the party started with a round of satisfying Blood Orange Margaritas. Make sure you use fresh blood oranges when making the purée. The juice is floral, tastes somewhere between grapefruit and raspberry, and provides just the right amount of sweet-tart flavor that intensifies the drink while the glass practically glows from the fruit's vibrant color.

1¼ ounces Santo (or Cabo Wabo) Blanco Tequila

½ ounce DeKuyper Blood Orange Liqueur

½ ounce triple sec (or any high-quality orange liqueur)

1½ ounces Blood Orange Purée (page 232)

½ ounce fresh lime juice

1 ounce Sweet & Sour Mix (page 235)

RIM:
Fresh lime and Tajín or Chipotle Sea Salt (page 235)

GARNISH:
Fresh lime wheel

Run a fresh lime wedge around the rim of a chilled margarita glass. Then roll the moistened rim in Tajín or Chipotle Sea Salt. Fill the glass with ice and set aside. In a cocktail shaker, add the tequila, Blood Orange Liqueur, triple sec, Blood Orange Purée, lime juice, and Sweet & Sour Mix. Shake well and pour into the prepared glass. Garnish with a fresh lime wheel and serve.

BRAZILIAN KISS

We all travel to Vegas for different reasons: To attend a conference or convention. The hope to strike it rich at the tables. And then there's the spectacular shows, concerts, and performances. But there's one activity that's louder than any slot machine alarm on the casino floor—hooking up. I'm telling ya, man, Vegas is the place for action. But when you're miles from the Strip, and it's just you and your well-stocked bar, kick back and smile because you're about to get lucky, too. Fill your glass with cachaça, St. Germain, strawberry, lime, and ginger ale, and watch as the sugarcane liqueur takes over. Cachaça is a Brazilian spirit with a slightly more robust and earthy flavor than rum. We serve this cocktail at Cabo Wabo and it's a hit. Just like Billy Joel's "Piano Man." You remember the verse: "There's an old man sittin' next to me / Makin' love to his tonic and gin"? One sip of this erotic sipper and you'll be makin' love to a mouthwatering Brazilian.

1 ounce cachaça

¼ ounce St. Germaine

¾ ounce Strawberry Purée (page 232)

½ ounce fresh lime juice

Ginger ale, as needed

GARNISH:
Fresh strawberry and mint leaf

In a cocktail shaker filled with ice, add the cachaça, St. Germaine, Strawberry Purée, and lime juice. Shake well and pour into a highball glass filled with ice. Top with ginger ale. Garnish with a fresh strawberry and mint leaf.

CABO MULES

SERVES
1

In the Splash of Aloha chapter, I introduced you to the Mint Macadamia Mule (page 058), my Hawaiian version of the classic Moscow Mule from the 1940s when vodka reigned supreme. Now that we're getting all wild and crazy in Vegas, I have to throw a whole pack of Mules at ya. For all you Redheads who've tied one on in Sin City, you know teamwork isn't just for playing sports and drafting spreadsheets. It's for drinking. And like my Cabo Wabo Cantina, I'm offering you a tasty trio of Cabo Mules to keep your party going. You choose the ride—tequila for a Mexican Mule, Jameson whisky for an Irish Mule, or Tito's vodka for an American Mule. Then I'll help you finish assembling the drinks with fresh lime and ginger beer so you can knock them back while jamming to some Vegas-themed tunes, like those from my Top Rock Countdown *radio show—Stripper Songs edition. What's more fun than drinking to "Girls Girls Girls" by Mötley Crüe, ZZ Top's "Legs," Def Leppard's "Pour Some Sugar on Me," and, one of my personal favs: "Sexy Little Thing" from Chickenfoot.*

1½ ounces alcohol (tequila, whisky, vodka; your choice)

½ ounce fresh lime juice

6 ounces ginger beer, or as needed

GARNISH:
Fresh lime wedge

Fill a rocks glass or copper mug with ice. Add the alcohol of choice and lime juice. Stir well and top with the ginger beer. Garnish with a fresh lime wedge and serve.

CABO ROCKIN' ICED TEA

I'll be the first to admit spiked iced teas are one of the quintessential drinks to cool down with when the sun's out, temperatures are soaring, and the party is bumping. In other words, the perfect Las Vegas cocktail. Forget all those sugary, watered-down versions of an iced tea served to you in plastic cups. To have one made right, you gotta head over to Cabo Wabo Las Vegas. We feature the Rockin' Iced Tea on our drink menu, which is made with Seagrams Sweet Tea Vodka, fresh mint, and lemonade. Tall and refreshing, this simple boozy tea goes down easy—as do all my signature drinks in this chapter. Now, let's break out the bar tools and make some of these invigorating teas. Then invite a few friends over to help you get through 'em. Because c'mon, man, cocktails should be sipped among friends, am I right?

1¼ ounce Seagrams Sweet Tea Vodka

6–8 fresh mint leaves

Fresh lemonade, as needed

GARNISH:
Fresh lemon wedge

Fill a Collins or highball glass with ice. Add the sweet tea vodka and mint leaves and top with lemonade. Stir well and garnish with a fresh lemon wedge.

COCORITA

You'll find a margarita on nearly every drink menu on the Strip but wait 'til you try this one. If you think the bold taste of tequila can't be tamed, take a sip of the Cocorita—another one of my signature Las Vegas cocktails at Cabo Wabo. Tequila and fresh lime juice are mellowed by cream of coconut for a deliciously sweet and tart beverage. I like to serve this frothy snow-white concoction—a cross between a Margarita and Pina Colada—shaken and poured on the rocks with a honey rim of freshly toasted coconut—just the way we serve 'em at the Cantina. This drink is pretty to look at, too. Sure, Mandalay Bay Beach may be the closest thing to sipping exotic cocktails in the South Pacific, but when you're miles away from Sin City, your home bar can easily convert to a Vegas-style tiki hut as you transport yourself and your guests from the desert to the tropics with this indulgent cocktail.

1¼ ounces Santo (or Cabo Wabo) Blanco Tequila

¼ ounce triple sec (or any high-quality orange liqueur)

1½ ounces Coco Lopez Cream of Coconut

½ ounce fresh lime juice

2 ounces Sweet & Sour Mix (page 235)

RIM:
Honey and shaved toasted coconut

GARNISH:
Fresh lime wheel

Roll the rim of a margarita glass in some honey. Then gently roll the honey rim in shaved toasted coconut. Fill the glass with ice and set aside. In a cocktail shaker, add the tequila, triple sec, cream of coconut, lime juice, and Sweet & Sour Mix. Shake well and pour into the prepared glass. Garnish with a fresh lime wheel and serve.

CUP OF GOLD

Vegas isn't all about limo rides, gambling, strip clubs, and star-studded shows—or maybe it is. For me, often the best times and coolest drinks are off the menu, and this favorite of mine is no exception. It starts by dusting off that bottle of champagne. You know, the one you haven't looked at for months. Pop that bottle and let's make what I consider an inventive cocktail and a definite upper. Why wouldn't it be, given rum, lime, honey, and sparkling wine? Whether you're after an exciting New Year's Eve drink or just wanting to toast a tiny victory, a minor win, or a twenty-four-hour triumph, this Vegas-inspired libation is always ready to please. Enjoy a Cup of Gold with my lick "One Sip" from the Livin' It Up *album. You know the lyrics—"Yeah man, here we go…One sip and you'll surrender…now shake it up and pour it tall." If you can, stick with a drier brut champagne. It seems to pair better when making fancy cocktails that incorporate the bubbly.*

2 ounces Sammy's Beach
Bar Platinum Rum

¾ ounce fresh lime juice

¾ ounce Monin Honey Syrup

2 ounces sparkling wine

GARNISH:
Fresh orange peel

In a cocktail shaker filled with ice, add the rum, lime juice, and honey syrup. Shake well and strain into a chilled tulip glass. Top with sparkling wine. Swath the rim with the fresh orange peel, then squeeze the oils into the drink and drop the peel into the cocktail.

JELLO SHOTS

Every now and then, I like to relive my youth. Go back to what it was like pursuing a career as a musician. And there's no better way to reminisce about those early years than with the most beloved party cocktail ever—the jello shot. This boozy little treat has been a staple of mine for as long as I can remember. I'd whip these up on Friday nights before the band came over to rehearse. I'd take them with me tubing down the river, and I always made sure there were plenty on the tour bus. I mean, who doesn't love a good jello shot? That's why I still feature them today on the Cabo Wabo Las Vegas drink menu. They're a fan favorite, simple to make, and the different colors and flavors make them extra fun. For a safe bet, start with vodka. It's the most neutral and versatile flavor. I also like to infuse rum with the tropical flavors of jello and tequila for citrus flavors, especially lime. Let's clear out some space in the fridge and make some of these party treats for your next Vegas shindig. I know they'll go quick, but in case if you're wondering, jello shots last about a week in the icebox before the gelatin starts breaking down and they get all funky in texture and taste. Best to make and consume them the same day.

1 package (3 ounces) JELL-O fruit flavor gelatin (lime, strawberry; your choice)

⅔ cup boiling water

⅔ cup cold water

⅔ cup alcohol (vodka, rum, tequila; your choice)

In a suitable bowl, add the JELL-O gelatin. Add the boiling water and stir until the gelatin is completely dissolved, about 2 minutes. Add the cold water and alcohol of choice. Stir well to incorporate. Divide the mixture into mini plastic disposable portion cups (about 2 ounces each) and refrigerate until firm.

KEY LIME MARTINI

As a kid, I craved anything with lime in it. Lime soda. Lime popsicles. Lime candies. As my palate matured and my music was taking off, I soon found limes were pretty rough on my vocal cords, especially right before a show. Now I only reach for lime when I'm not belting out tunes. I'm also not much of a dessert guy, which you may know by now, but every once in a while, especially when the weather heats up like it obviously does in Vegas, my tastebuds beg me for a little lime and graham cracker. This leads me to either a slice of freshly-baked key lime pie made with real key limes or a Key Lime Martini, which we feature on the Cabo Wabo Las Vegas bar menu. One sip and, man, and it's key lime pie in liquid form. Our sugar-eyed fans rave about its decadent and delicious qualities. Many ask us why we list this martini as a signature drink and not as a dessert special. If you're ready for a cocktail that's rich and creamy and tart and tropical, you gotta make one of these. I bet you inhale instead of sip. It's that delicious. Just like the chorus of Van Halen's "Ice Cream Man"— "Stop me when I'm passin' by. I'm your ice cream man. They say all my flavors are guaranteed to satisfy...."

½ ounce Sammy's Beach Bar Platinum Rum

1½ ounces KeKe Key Lime Pie Cream Liqueur

½ ounce banana liqueur

½ ounce Coco Lopez Cream of Coconut

½ ounce fresh lime juice

RIM:
Honey and crushed graham cracker

GARNISH:
Fresh lime wheel

Roll the rim of a chilled martini glass in some honey. Then gently roll the honey rim in crushed graham cracker and set the glass aside. Fill a cocktail shaker with ice and add the rum, KeKe Key Lime Pie Cream Liqueur, banana liqueur, cream of coconut, and lime juice. Shake well and strain into the prepared glass. Garnish with a fresh lime wheel and serve.

KIR ROYALE

Nothing says classy Las Vegas vacation like sipping Red Head Rum, chilled champagne, and a lemon twist from an elegant flute on a balcony or terrace. For all you classy people out there who love classy drinks at home, this one's for you. You can even pretend you're clinking glasses at the Skyfall Cocktail Lounge on the sixty-fourth floor of the Delano. Sidenote: If you want to experience the best in champagne while in Vegas, there's at least a half dozen places on the Strip to sip some really good stuff. But if you're miles away and ready to dress up your bubbly as part of a fabulous cocktail, try the Kir Royale. This sinful sipper is festively fizzy and tart with an underlying macadamia flavor thanks to the exotic-tasting rum. It's the backbone to this exquisite cocktail.

1 ounce Sammy's Red Head Rum, divided

4 ounces chilled champagne

GARNISH:
Fresh lemon twist

Add half the rum to a chilled champagne flute. Slowly add the chilled champagne until ½-inch from the top. Top with the remaining rum. Garnish with a fresh lemon twist.

LEMON DROP MARTINI

SERVES
1

If you're wary of starting your Vegas party with a shot of booze—like the Lemon Shot on page 146—simply transform that little shooter into a delicious cocktail. Just pour into a martini glass rimmed with some sugar, add some ice, and finish it off with a lemon garnish for an equally satisfying Lemon Drop Martini. I find this to be a great vacation drink and a terrific choice when I want a cocktail with a bit of pucker and a hint of sweetness. The key to a well-made lemon drop is the right balance between sweet and sour. That means your cocktail should taste refreshingly tart, not cloyingly sweet. A lukewarm martini is no fun either, so shake, shake, shake the heck out of this drink before pouring. If you want, go the extra mile and chill your glass beforehand. Now parlay this with some good music, tasty apps, and those tiny firefly-looking lights and you have yourself a swanky Las Vegas bar scene in no time.

2 ounces Sammy's Beach Bar Platinum Rum

1 ounce limoncello

2 ounces Sweet & Sour Mix (page 235)

RIM:
Fresh lemon and sugar

GARNISH:
Fresh lemon wedge

Run a fresh lemon wedge around the rim of a chilled martini glass. Then roll the moistened rim in sugar and set the glass aside. In a cocktail shaker filled with ice, add the rum, limoncello, and Sweet & Sour Mix. Shake well and strain into the prepared glass. Garnish with a fresh lemon wedge and serve.

LEMON SHOT

Some of the most popular drinks at Cabo Wabo Las Vegas are shots. Hell, they're portable. They go down quickly. They're potent, and they get the job done. I believe a well-made shot—like this one that tastes like its name—can set the mood for the evening and is a great icebreaker, especially on date night with "Your Love Is Driving Me Crazy" (from Three Lock Box*) spinning in the background. The little cousin to my Lemon Drop Martini (page 144), this refreshing shooter is simple, clean, and delicious. It's also great for any occasion thanks to the tropical rum and the tanginess of the limoncello and Sweet & Sour Mix. But, man, don't let this shot fool you—they're sneaky little critters. Too many and you might find yourself dancing on the table, revisiting the moonwalk, or waking up on the bathroom floor.*

1 ounce Sammy's Beach Bar
Platinum Rum

½ ounce limoncello

1 ounce Sweet & Sour Mix
(page 235)

GARNISH:
Fresh lemon wedge and
spoonful of sugar
on the side

In a cocktail shaker filled with ice, add the rum, limoncello, and Sweet & Sour Mix. Shake extra well and strain into an extra-large shot glass. For added flavor, take a bite of lemon and lick of sugar before drinking.

LITTLE RED DEVIL

When I need a cool aperitif on a hot summer night, I'll stir up this colorful sipper. This is my riff on the Negroni, and man are they gorgeous, refreshing, and easy to make. Definitely one of my warm weather mainstays, especially when I'm here in Vegas. Instead of gin, I swap out the base spirit with the smoky-agave flavors of mezquila. I find the mezcal-tequila blend really complements the bitter, bold flavors of the striking red Campari, which should always stay put. That's because this Italian spirit is the one ingredient that all Negronis have in common. Stir together with ice, add a slice of blood red orange, and you've just created a glass filled with youthful sophistication. It's my answer to Vegas happy hours and they're sure to impress the guests.

1 ounce Santo Mezquila

1 ounce Campari

GARNISH:
Fresh blood orange slice

Add some ice to a chilled rocks glass then add the mezquila and Campari. Stir well to combine and garnish with a fresh blood orange slice.

NUTTY RED HEAD

Every now and then, I find myself craving dessert. One night I had a hankering for something sweet after an impromptu performance at Cabo Wabo Las Vegas—I sang The Beatles' "Birthday" (featured on Sammy Hagar & The Circle's Space Between*) to a woman who just turned twenty-one. I dipped into the Wabo kitchen and quickly found a banana, a container of Häagen-Dazs Vanilla Swiss Almond Ice Cream (my favorite), some almond butter, and a bottle of my Red Head Rum. All of a sudden, I'm staring at these ingredients and thinking, "I bet if Elvis were here, he'd grab this, too," (although he would've likely fried his banana in butter). My fellow Redheads, I give you the Vegas-Elvis inspired Nutty Red Head—and it's to die for. My buddy Guy Fieri will talk you into mixing it all up in a blender for an incredible late-night milkshake with a kick. Personally, I like savoring each ingredient separately. Your choice. And if you add a little whipped cream and a sprinkling of nuts on top—milkshake or not—boom! You have a delicious treat with a zing to wrap up your night!*

2 scoops Häagen-Dazs Vanilla Swiss Almond Ice Cream

1 ripe banana, peeled and sliced into small pieces

1 tablespoon crunchy almond butter

2 ounces Sammy's Beach Bar Red Head Rum

GARNISH: Whipped cream and nuts, optional

In a bowl or large coffee cup, add the ice cream, then arrange the sliced bananas on top. Add the almond butter on top of the bananas, then pour the rum over the ice cream, bananas, and almond butter. Top with whipped cream and nuts, if desired.

PEACH BLENDED BELLINI

This blended bellini recipe is my riff on the classic Venetian cocktail, which I make with tequila and fresh seasonal peaches instead of traditional champagne and white peaches. For those who may not know the difference, a mimosa is made with orange juice while a bellini is made with peaches. And I find the color of bright-orange peaches much more pronounced than the soft pink hue of those white varieties. Regardless of which peaches you choose, peach bellinis are perfection in a glass. This frosty tequila adaptation, which can be described as part bellini, part margarita, is no exception. The juicy peach flavor gives this simple concoction a boost of sunshine, and the kick of tequila and the cool frozen slushy texture makes it one of my all-time favorite Vegas cocktails. Enjoy one out on your veranda or at your re-created Las Vegas pool party ala the Encore Beach Club. I promise this magically colorful cocktail will be the centerpiece of your next glitzy gathering—especially if you have "Trust Fund Baby" from Sammy Hagar & The Circle jamming in the background.

1½ ounces Santo Blanco Tequila

3 ounces Peach Purée (page 232)

GARNISH:
Fresh peach slice

In a bar or kitchen blender, add the tequila, Peach Purée, and a handful of crushed ice. Blend until smooth and frothy. Pour into a chilled champagne flute and garnish with a fresh peach slice.

RED HEADED ITALIANO

SERVES 1

If you ever spent time in Las Vegas during the summer, you know it's scorching hot down here. Luckily, the Entertainment Capital of the World is equipped with plenty of ways to keep you cool when the temperatures spike above one hundred. And that includes ice-cold beverages to beat the heat. Named after the natural beauty of redheaded women all over Italy—and Las Vegas, of course—this tropically inspired, coffee-influenced cocktail is attractive and frigid in its own right. The macadamia-infused Red Head Rum brings out the ginger color like the volcanic eruptions at the Mirage. A splash of Ristretto Coffee Liqueur awakens the senses with full-flavors of roasted coffee bean and chocolate. And the Beach Bar Rum adds enough coconut and banana notes to anchor this delicious twist on the Piña Colada. All that's left now is for you to close your eyes and pretend you're sipping one of these Italianos on the Strip.

1 ounce Sammy's Beach Bar
Platinum Rum

¾ ounce Ristretto
Coffee Liqueur

2 ounces Coco López Piña
Colada Mix

1 ounce Sammy's
Red Head Rum

GARNISH:
Fresh pineapple wedge,
strawberry, paper umbrella

In a bar or kitchen blender, add the Beach Bar Platinum Rum, coffee liqueur, piña colada mix, and some ice. Blend until smooth. In a chilled hurricane glass, add the Red Head Rum, then pour the contents from the blender into the glass. Garnish with a wedge of fresh pineapple, strawberry, and paper umbrella.

SANTO REVELATION

Las Vegas is, and always will be, a drinking town. No surprise more than forty million visitors flock to the desert and the river of booze that keeps the masses lubricated for the big conference, bachelorette party, or poker tournament. Of course, nothing would ever happen if the cocktails in the City of Lost Wages weren't sinfully superb. Indulge yourself with a Santo Revelation, an ideal drink that reflects the glitz and glamour of Vegas. This bright and sophisticated drink is simple with flavors that are seemingly meant for each other. Think of the Santo Revelation as a cross between a margarita and a Mexican Mule, sassed up with passion fruit and pomegranate, and served tall in a Collins glass with a slice of ginger kissing the rim. A group of revelers looking to score in Sin City will likely spend a fortune on bottle service and a table to impress. At home, all you need is a little bartending prowess and delicious cocktails like this one to set the night on fire.

2 slices fresh ginger root

1 fresh lime wedge

1 ounce passion fruit purée

1½ ounces Santo Mezquila

2 ounces ginger beer

¼ ounce pomegranate syrup (or grenadine)

GARNISH:
Fresh ginger slice

In a cocktail shaker, add the two slices of fresh ginger root, lime wedge, and passion fruit purée. Using a muddler, gently (yet firmly) muddle the ingredients. Add the mezquila. Fill the shaker with ice and shake. Strain the entire contents into a Collins glass filled with ice. Top with the ginger beer and slowly add the pomegranate syrup (or grenadine) so it slowly sinks to the bottom. Garnish with a slice of fresh ginger and serve.

STRAWBERITA

Let's face it: Las Vegas is a city that likes to get creative. It's also where vacationers come to get away. Now you can, too, in the comfort of your own home with this delicious margarita. The strawberry marg is one of our most popular margaritas here at Cabo Wabo—we call it the Strawberita—and making one from scratch is a breeze. It requires the holy trinity of tequila, fresh lime juice, and orange liqueur. With this one, I shake and don't blend. Then I add some homemade strawberry syrup, simple syrup, and sliced berries. Fresh strawberries are a must because it ensures a fresher taste than those store-bought margarita mixes. You can also use frozen berries. They come in handy when you want to enjoy this fruity cocktail year-round. If you really want to impress, serve these drinks with some Vegas ambience and the driving soundtrack from Space Between *with The Circle.*

1½ ounces Santo
Blanco Tequila

2 ounces fresh lime juice

1 ounce triple sec (or any
high-quality orange liqueur)

1 ounce Strawberry Syrup
(page 234)

1 ounce Simple Syrup
(page 233)

3 freshly sliced strawberries

GARNISH:
Fresh strawberries and
lime wheel

In a cocktail shaker filled with ice, add the tequila, lime juice, triple sec, Strawberry Syrup, Simple Syrup, and sliced strawberries. Shake well and strain into a rocks glass or brandy snifter filled with ice. Garnish with fresh strawberries and a lime wheel.

TAMARIND MARGARITA

Here's a drink every tequila fan needs to try. It's a captivating flavor combination, with the sweet and sour from the tamarind syrup pairing wonderfully off the tequila. It's the perfect harmony. And what the heck is tamarind? It's a unique fruit from the tamarind tree that's used in Indian, Mexican, and Mediterranean cuisine—very eclectic, like the bars and eateries on the Vegas Strip. Tamarind is very sour but sweetens as the fruit ripens. When it comes to adding tamarind to drinks you can go several ways. For this recipe, I prefer to use premade tamarind syrup—much easier than making it from scratch. You can also mix up some syrup using tamarind concentrate powder—both are available at specialty stores and online. Like many of my margaritas served here at Cabo Wabo Las Vegas, I prefer to serve this marg on the rocks and in a glass accented with a chili pepper rim to set it over the top. Add some tequila, triple sec, tamarind, lime, and Sweet & Sour to a shaker while my old tune "Straight to the Top" from the Sweet Machine *album jams through your Bluetooth speaker. Shake and pour, and you got yourself one extraordinary cocktail that's a nice change of pace.*

1¼ ounces Santo (or Cabo Wabo) Blanco Tequila

¼ ounce triple sec (or any high-quality orange liqueur)

1½ ounces tamarind syrup (or from concentrated drink mix)

½ ounce fresh lime juice

2 ounces Sweet & Sour Mix (page 235)

RIM:
Fresh lime and Tajín or Chipotle Sea Salt (page 235)

GARNISH:
Fresh lime wheel

Run a fresh lime wedge around the rim of a chilled margarita glass. Then roll the moistened rim in Tajín or Chipotle Sea Salt. Fill the glass with ice and set aside. In a cocktail shaker, add the tequila, triple sec, tamarind syrup, lime juice, and Sweet & Sour Mix. Shake well and pour into the prepared glass. Garnish with a fresh lime wheel and serve.

VOJITO

This is my Vegas version of the popular mojito, and I dig the fruity spin on it. Served up as a featured special at Cabo Wabo, it's another one of my go-to's when hitting the Strip. Often, I'll bring the band up from Cabo Wabo in San Lucas, Mexico— I've probably played with them more than any other band I've been in. They know about twenty of my songs, especially Toby Keith's "I Love This Bar," which always gets a roar from the crowd, and we know like twenty of other people's songs. I'll fly them up to Vegas for the whole week and we just jam and play music. We also like to throw a big party while in town, and these Vojitos always make the cocktail list. The secret is the blackberry vodka, produced by Pinnacle in France's Cognac Region. Not only is it distilled five times for exceptional balance and smoothness, but the light, clean blackberry offsets the tartness of the lime, which, like I said before, can be rough on my vocal cords right before a show. I tell ya, one sip of this refreshing cocktail, and you'll find yourself lounging in a warm blackberry patch on a blissful summer day. Feel free to change up the Vojito by swapping the blackberry for other vodka flavors like peach, raspberry, citrus, or tropical punch.

3 fresh lime or lemon wedges

6–7 fresh mint leaves

3 fresh blackberries

6 fresh blueberries

¾ ounce Simple Syrup (page 233)

2 ounces Pinnacle Blackberry Vodka

2 ounces soda water

GARNISH:
Fresh mint sprig, lime wedge, blackberry

In a cocktail shaker, add the lime or lemon wedges, mint leaves, blackberries, blueberries, and simple syrup. Using a muddler, gently (yet firmly) muddle the ingredients. Fill the shaker with some ice and add the vodka. Shake for about 10 seconds, then pour (do not strain) into a Collins glass filled with ice. Top with soda water and garnish with the fresh mint sprig, lime wedge, and blackberry.

WABO BOWL

If Las Vegas had a bucket list for cocktails, my Wabo Bowl would be on it. It's a giant, forty-ounce cocktail featuring a bunch of booze, fruit juices, and garnishes. I tell ya, the Wabo Bowl is as much fun to drink as it is to look at—like all the beautiful people on the Strip. Listen, man, if you're a fan of those mega punch-style cocktails like the Scorpion Bowl, you'll dig the Wabo Bowl. Make one for your next party, and I bet your living room lounge with the fireplace and that big rug of yours will look even better. All you need are the ingredients below and a bunch of good friends to share it with. Sip one while cranking the volume on "24635" from my Cosmic Universal Fashion *album. If you forget the chorus, it goes a little something like this…. "24365 Gonna party now. 24365 Kick it up. 24365 To the middle now. Flip flop, tank top, 'round the clock, nonstop baby, Hey!" I don't know about you, but I'm ready to dive into my Wabo Bowl.*

2 ounces Absolut Mandrin Vodka

2 ounces gin

2 ounces Malibu Rum

2 ounces triple sec (or any high-quality orange liqueur)

2 ounces peach schnapps

2 ounces Damiana liqueur

1½ ounces fresh lime juice

4 ounces cranberry juice

4 ounces fresh orange juice

4 ounces fresh pineapple juice

GARNISH:
Cherries, fresh orange slices, lime slices, gummy worms, paper umbrellas, multicolored flexible straws

Fill an approximately 40-ounce cocktail fishbowl with ice (this size will allow room to spare for garnishes and any other accoutrements like umbrellas and gummies). Add the vodka, gin, rum, triple sec, peach schnapps, Damiana liqueur, lime juice, and cranberry, orange, and pineapple juices. Mix well until incorporated. Garnish with the cherries, fresh fruit slices, and gummy worms. Add the paper umbrellas and straws and serve.

TINSELTOWN TWISTS

(WITH CLEVELAND PRE-FUNK)

I WAS ABOUT FIFTEEN WHEN I PICKED UP A GUITAR AND LEARNED MY FIRST SONG: "I WANNA HOLD YOUR HAND" BY THE BEATLES. From then on, I knew playing music, singing, and writing songs was the only thing I wanted to do. I had big dreams, and I worked my ass off to make them come true. Fast forward forty-five years from those first chords, and there I am onstage in Cleveland singing "Why Can't This Be Love" just after being inducted into the Rock 'n' Roll Hall of Fame as a member of Van Halen. All I could think was, *damned if I wasn't right, even way back then.*

Music ended up taking me everywhere I wanted to go, but even I didn't know I wanted to make rum and tequila or open cantinas and beach bars. One thing just led to another—but if I trace the journey backward, it's fair to say I ended up in Hollywood by way of Cleveland, so this cocktail tasting tour ends the same way: in Tinseltown, with a Cleveland pre-funk.

This chapter features an eclectic list of cocktails fit for Hollywood's brightest stars. Bold, creative, unique flavors to pair with silver screens, technicolor dreams, and fantasies of fame and fortune. They're mostly inspired by the drinks at Cabo Wabo's Hollywood location, along with a couple of hard-rockin' cocktails from Sammy's Beach Bar & Grill at Hopkins Airport in Cleveland. They'll keep you flying (first class) to your final destination.

Spend a little time in Hollywood, and you start to see rock stars and movie stars everywhere: at every red carpet, at every industry party, and at your favorite coffee shop. On one hand, celebrity sightings are so common it's hard to get star struck; and on the other it's pretty inspiring to be surrounded by so much talent, hard work, and ambition.

The energy is something else in Hollywood, which makes sense when you think about how much people sacrifice when they're trying to make it to the top. They'll work and sweat and try and fail and try again, chasing dreams that few people ever achieve. There's something to be said for waking up every day with the hope that the right people caught last night's show, or that today will be the day you'll finally get your big break. So how do you capture that kind of energy in an at-home Hollywood bar?

Just follow your passion, because anything goes in Hollywood. The space you create can be anything from a designer label, Oscar party to an effortlessly cool, low-key spot where glamour is a given and everyone gets the celebrity treatment.

You say Los Angeles and everyone thinks movies—but it's home to as many iconic bands and historic clubs as sound stages. So why not make your Hollywood bar a dark, gritty rock club with speakers blasting music by L.A. bands like Guns N' Roses, Mötley Crüe, Rage Against the Machine, and Dokken, one of the bands who opened for Van Halen during the 1988 Monsters of Rock tour. I've played alongside all these guys at one point or another, and I still count a few among my best friends. Throw on some classic Montrose, Van Halen, or your favorites from my solo albums and you'll feel like you're right there with us.

It makes perfect sense to let your favorite music decide the kind of atmosphere you're after. Take a cue from the Troubadour, the historic L.A. club where it seems like everyone who's anyone either got their big break, made their U.S. debut, or played shows people still remember. Everyone from Bob Dylan to The Doors to Metallica; Nina Simone to Carole King; Elton John to Pearl Jam; Miles Davis to Willie Nelson. The list doesn't stop—and if you're throwing the right kind of party, neither will the music and cocktails. But there's all kinds of ways to do it right.

If you love the beach, like I do, maybe create a sun-bleached surf shack with the Beach Boys on heavy rotation. Serve up a menu of summer-fun cocktails including my Cali Sunset, Strawberry Surf, Cucumber Smash, and Summer Splash. By now, your bar should be pretty well stocked. A quick trip to your local market for fresh strawberries, tangerines, oranges, limes, and cucumbers, and you're all set to create bright, beautiful cocktails as refreshing as the California sand and surf, and as welcome as a bonfire when the sun goes down.

If a surfing safari's not your style, think tiki. There's nothing more Hollywood than a bar modeled after Don the Beachcomber, the Hollywood restaurant that first started the tiki trend in 1933. Take a cue from the movies and create an island paradise wherever you live. Let some steel guitar and traditional drums set the mood and you'll be slinging rum cocktails all night—including the Hot Tiki Toddy, as warm and exotic as the

lush, other-worldly vibe you've designed for your guests.

Into the folk rock made popular by '60s L.A. bands like the Byrds and Buffalo Springfield? Make your bar a midcentury shrine to California cool. Clean modern lines, a nod to car culture, and specialty cocktails like the Sweet Hitchhiker with its simple, delicious twist on a classic rum and cola. A Southbound Greyhound gives you the same carefree feeling as a shades-on, windows-down cruise through the desert; but if it's thrills you're after, try the five-spirit, five-mixer Can't Drive 55—it's the cocktail version of a sports-car pushing the limits on the open road. Just make sure no one's actually driving after any of these.

If jazz is up your alley, your basement bar could just as easily be a speakeasy modeled after the original Hollywood Frolic room, which—a couple decades after finally going legal—hosted the Academy Awards after-*after* party in the early '50s, when Sinatra was a regular. Serve up some of my California signatures from this chapter and maybe make the Higher Spirit on page 190 your bartender's special: a mezquila, aperol, chartreuse concoction as mesmerizing as the swing and blue notes floating from your speakers. It's an improvisation of my own, with a flavor profile the likes of which your guests have never tasted.

Three chapters into the *Cocktail Hit Set List* and I'm betting you can already make ten different margaritas while chatting up your guests, and just as many rum-based beauties. Now's when you add dry vermouth if you don't already have it, plus vodka. Four bottles if you've got room: Black & Blue Devotion, Hangar 1 Chipotle, Deep Eddy Ruby Red, and your favorite unflavored brand. Now you can mix up my take on a spicy Bloody Mary, a berry-blasted hard lemonade, and about a dozen other drinks including simple riffs and twist on screwdrivers, classic martinis, mules, cosmos, and lemon drops. If you're up for adding amaretto and yellow chartreuse, you'll be able to shake up a few more of my personal favorites and offer your VIP guests a few drinks they'd never think to make at home.

If I can leave you with one piece of advice, it's that a great cocktail menu doesn't have to be fussy, and a great bartender doesn't need to know every drink ever invented. The best bartender's trick is to make people feel special. It's that simple. Everyone's an A-lister when they walk into your bar.

Okay, I lied; here's a second piece of advice. Follow your dreams, be they big or small. I can say from experience, they almost always take you someplace you'd never have planned or expected. And that place is some kind of wonderful.

Cheers, my friends.

HANGAR 1 CHIPOTLE MARY

SERVES
1

Let's kick off our final party in this book with a pre-funk in Cleveland, and I have two cocktails worthy of the occasion. The first you'll find on virtually every table come Sunday at Sammy Hagar's Beach Bar & Grill inside Cleveland Hopkins International Airport. Cool thing is profits from my Grill go to area food banks and children's charities through the Hagar Family Foundation. For this all-American cocktail, I prefer Hangar 1 (not Hagar) small-batch Chipotle Vodka. Hangar 1 harvests fresh chipotles from a sustainable organic farm. The result is an extraordinarily unique vodka, perfect for this spicy sipper. I also like to use a good-quality pre-made mix because, let's be honest, the Bloody Mary can be a labor-intensive drink, and I like keeping it simple. At the Grill, we garnish our Chipotle Mary with a traditional celery stalk and a skewer of olive, cherry tomato, and a wedge of lime.

2 ounces Hangar 1 Chipotle Vodka

4 ounces Bloody Mary mix (such as Zing Zang, Mr. & Mrs. T's, or McClure's)

GARNISH: Fresh celery stalk and skewer of fresh lime, olive, and cherry tomato

In one cocktail shaker filled with ice, add the vodka and Bloody Mary mix. Next, place a strainer, like a Hawthorn strainer, over the top of the shaker and pour/strain immediately into another shaker that's empty (with no strainer). Now pour the contents back into the first shaker through the strainer that has the ice. Now back into the empty shaker. Do this back and forth for about 15 seconds. This is called the roll and throw method (like we used on page 050); transferring the cocktail back and forth from one shaker to the next allows the drink to chill in one shaker while the other shaker mixes the cocktail without too much dilution or aeration. Now, pour/strain one last time into a highball glass filled with ice. Garnish with a fresh celery stalk and skewer of fresh lime, olive, and cherry tomato.

RED ROCKER

Redheads, I feel I'm the luckiest man in the world. That's because, aside from my beautiful family and health, every year I get to spend my birthday bash hanging with my friends and fans while performing my favorite licks, including some of my early songs like "Red" from The Essential Red Collection. *More times than not, I'm holding a Red Rocker when it comes to making the celebratory toast. This drink is another sipper well suited for pre-funking. Many have nicknamed it "Sammy's Special Birthday Cocktail." The ravishing red swig of tequila, pomegranate, and lime is also a sure bet here at Cleveland's Sammy's Beach Bar & Grill, just like the Hangar 1 Chipotle Mary. I like playing up the red color of this drink with equally bright red cocktail napkins. Now, before we rush to the gate and jetset over to Hollywood and get all glammed up with an eclectic menu of cinematic and red-carpet delights, let's take a moment to honor the city of Cleveland, which is also home to the Rock 'n' Roll Hall of Fame where I got inducted. As many of you know, I've been playing Cleveland since 1972 with Montrose, and the city and its passionate fans have always been good to me. With our freshly made Red Rockers in hand, let's all raise our glass to Cleveland—the birthplace of rock and roll.*

2 ounces Cabo Wabo Blanco Tequila

1 ounce Monin Pomegranate Syrup

1 fresh lime wedge

GARNISH: Fresh lime wedge

In a cocktail shaker filled with ice, add the tequila and pomegranate syrup, then squeeze the lime wedge into the shaker and drop in the wedge. Shake well and strain into a small cocktail glass. Garnish with a fresh lime wedge.

BLACK & BLUE LEMONADE

SERVES
1

"Welcome to Hollywood! What's your dream?" It's a classic line from the movie Pretty Woman, *which best sums up this city. Hollywood—home to the American film and television industry, and an industry that elicits images of fame and fortune. This city is also filled with sights and attractions that pay tribute to the entertainment biz and its larger-than-life persona, from studio tours and theme parks to red-carpet premieres on Sunset Strip and Hollywood Boulevard. Of course, no trip to the City of Angels is complete without a stop at Cabo Wabo Cantina. Whether you're visiting for the first time or are a lifelong Angeleno, the Cantina is where it's at—and where most of the cocktails in this chapter can be found, including this knockout potion that you'll be serving up at your next Hollywood-themed cookout or dinner party at home. Inspired by spiked lemonades, the Black & Blue Lemonade is summer in a glass. Just add some Black & Blue Devotion Vodka—made with crisp, zesty California blueberries and sweet, rich Oregon blackberries—to freshly-made lemonade with muddled berries for a refreshingly sweet zing that will excite your A-list guests each and every time.*

2 fresh blackberries

2 fresh blueberries

1½ ounces Black & Blue Devotion Vodka

1 ounce fresh lemon juice

2 ounces Simple Syrup (page 233)

2 ounces cold water

GARNISH:
Fresh lemon wheel

Add the fresh berries to a cocktail shaker. Using a muddler, gently (yet firmly) muddle the berries. Add the vodka, lemon juice, Simple Syrup, and water. Shake well and pour the entire contents into an old fashioned or rocks glass. Garnish with a fresh lemon wheel.

CABO TINI

Another one of my popular and creative cocktails on the Cabo Wabo Hollywood drink menu is the Cabo Tini. Crafted with tequila, orange liqueur, fresh lime, and vermouth, this kicky version of the classic martini is smooth and tangy with bright citrus flavor. It's a terrific way to sip your favorite tequila, and they're simple to make because it's basically a margarita, but with vermouth, served as a martini. The garnish and V-shaped glass create the martini ambience, and the savory flavors and smooth finish will take your love of margaritas to a new, shaken level. Friends, let's get our shakers ready and make some of these 'tinis as we start partying Hollywood style. Let's also turn up Pink Floyd's old riff "Double O Bo" in which Bo Didley drinks martinis so dry that the shaker bursts and Bo dies of thirst. Don't worry, you won't be dying of thirst with these tasty beverages in hand.

2 ounces Cabo Wabo
Blanco Tequila

½ ounce triple sec (or any
high-quality orange liqueur)

½ ounce dry vermouth

2 ounces Sweet & Sour Mix
(page 235)

RIM:
Fresh lime and sea salt

GARNISH:
Fresh lime wheel

Run a fresh lime wedge around the rim of a chilled martini glass. Then roll the moistened rim in sea salt and set the glass aside. Next, add the tequila, triple sec, dry vermouth, and Sweet & Sour Mix to a cocktail shaker filled with ice. Shake well and strain into the prepared glass. Garnish with a fresh lime wheel.

CALI SUNSET

If you've ever spent time here on the California coast, you've seen the sun dip over the horizon while the sky transforms into a stunning canvas filled with splashes of color. These California sunsets often remind me of vibrant paintings and the hit "California Dreamin'" by The Mamas & The Papas. Enjoying a fiery sunset out west is also one of the most relaxing ways to end an evening—or start one—depending on how you roll. For me, my definition of California dreamin' is holding a Cali Sunset in my hand and gawking at the thick puffs of clouds that churn from periwinkle blue to flaming orangey pink. This beautiful, refreshingly fruity cocktail represents the radiant colors of the sunsets as they cast their spectacular hues on palm tree–lined streets, ocean shores, and many of those iconic California piers that stretch out over the sea. Fine tequila, orange liqueur, and sweet and sour infused with strawberry, tangerine, and cucumber. It's my riff on the Tequila Sunrise. Let's drink.

2 fresh strawberries, washed and hulled

⅓ fresh tangerine, peeled and segmented

1 (2-inch) piece fresh cucumber, peeled

1½ ounces Cabo Wabo Blanco Tequila

½ ounce triple sec (or any high-quality orange liqueur)

3 ounces Sweet & Sour Mix (page 235)

RIM:
Fresh lime and sea salt

GARNISH:
Fresh lime wedge

Run a fresh lime wedge around the rim of an old fashioned or rocks glass. Then roll the moistened rim in sea salt and set the glass aside. Next, add the fresh strawberries, tangerine, and cucumber to a cocktail shaker. Using a muddler, gently (yet firmly) muddle the ingredients and then fill the shaker with ice. Add the tequila, triple sec, and Sweet & Sour Mix. Shake well and pour the entire contents into the prepared glass. Garnish with a fresh lime wedge.

CAN'T DRIVE 55

SERVES
1

This signature of mine, a top-seller at Cabo Wabo Hollywood, is named after my Billboard hit, "I Can't Drive 55." In the summer of '84, that tune blasted out of the Kraco speakers of virtually every Camaro in America. For those who don't know the story—I know my Redheads do—a cop pulled me over for doing 62 on a four-lane road on my way to Lake Placid. I remember him stepping up to my window and saying, "We give tickets around here for over 60," to which I replied, "I can't drive 55." When he returned to his car to write me a ticket, I grabbed a paper and pen from the glovebox and began scribbling the lyrics. When I got to Lake Placid, I finished the song. Enjoy a Can't Drive 55 cocktail featuring platinum rum, tequila, vodka, gin, and amaretto blended with cranberry, orange, pineapple, lime, and grenadine. It pairs well with the verse: "When I drive that slow, you know it's hard to steer. And I can't get my car out of second gear. What used to take two hours now takes all day. Huh! It took me sixteen hours to get to L.A."

½ ounce Sammy's Beach Bar Platinum Rum

½ ounce Cabo Wabo Blanco Tequila

½ ounce vodka

½ ounce gin

½ ounce amaretto

½ ounce cranberry juice

½ ounce fresh orange juice

½ ounce fresh pineapple juice

½ ounce fresh lime juice

1 splash grenadine

GARNISH:
Fresh orange wedge and maraschino cherry

In a cocktail shaker filled with ice, add the rum, tequila, vodka, gin, and amaretto followed by the cranberry, orange, pineapple, and lime juices. Finish with a splash of grenadine. Shake well and pour the entire contents into an old fashioned or rocks glass. Garnish with a fresh orange wedge and maraschino cherry.

CRAZY HAGAR

For those cinema buffs out there like me, I enjoy classic Hollywood films, such as The Seven Year Itch with Marilyn Monroe. In the movie, there's a scene when the blonde bombshell dunks her potato chips into a glass of champagne. At first, this struck me as odd. The second time I watched the movie, I realized the scene represents the marriage of high and low society; a cinematic example of the enduring principle that opposites attract. When it comes to creations like the Crazy Hagar, made with rum and beer, what might not seem right together actually works— just like Marilyn's chips and bubbly. This drink is my riff on the mojito, and it's a marvelous cocktail to assemble the next time you're hosting a movie night. The Crazy Hagar also pairs well with happy hours, afternoons by the pool, and weekend grill-outs. Vibrant and lovely, the Crazy Hagar is another one you should add to your Hollywood party repertoire.

10–12 fresh mint leaves

1½ ounces Sammy's Beach Bar Rum

1 ounce fresh lime juice

¾ ounce Amoretti Rock Candy Syrup

Kasteel Rouge Lambic beer, cold

GARNISH:
Fresh lemon wedge

Add the mint to a chilled highball glass. Using a muddler, gently (yet firmly) muddle the mint and fill the shaker with ice. Add the rum, lime juice, and rock candy syrup. Stir well and top with the Lambic beer. Garnish with a fresh lemon wedge and serve.

CUCUMBER SMASH

This is my twist on the Skinny Rita (page 202) with, you guessed it, cucumber. Adding cucumber makes a margarita like this one more refreshing in flavor without adding extra sugar. I also believe margs are best when they're homemade, and I have yet to find a pre-made margarita mix I like. They're all too sweet and artificial tasting. To me, nothing beats fresh lime and, in this case, fresh cucumber. And since we're counting calories when it comes to the Skinny Rita and versions thereof, Hollywood socialites and home bartenders will be pleased to know my Cucumber Smash has only 135 calories. Heck, your mouth and waist will think you made a juice cleanse. When I sip this drink, I feel like the cucumber juice is hydrating me, even though it's a cocktail, and the lime offers a nice, tart bite that complements the cuke. This drink special, authentic in flavor, is served up daily at Cabo Wabo Hollywood, but I encourage you to make them at home while rockin' out to my single "Let me Take You There." All together now, "I'm a sunshine stalker. Hodaddy wave watcher. Heaven's door knocker. Blue, white, and red rocker!"

2 (2-inch) pieces fresh cucumber, peeled

2 ounces Cabo Wabo Blanco Tequila

¾ ounce agave nectar

1 fresh lime, cut in half

Soda water, as needed

RIM:
Fresh lime and sea salt

GARNISH:
Fresh lime wedge

Run a fresh lime wedge around the rim of an old fashioned or rocks glass. Then roll the moistened rim in sea salt and set the glass aside. Next, add the cucumber to a cocktail shaker. Using a muddler, gently (yet firmly) muddle the cucumber and fill the shaker with ice. Add the tequila and agave nectar. Next, squeeze the juice from both halves of the lime into the shaker and drop one of the squeezed lime halves into the shaker (discarding the other half). Shake well and pour the entire contents into the prepared glass. Top with soda water and garnish with a fresh lime wedge.

HIGHER SPIRIT

Did you know the world-famous Hollywood Walk of Fame, where the stars of Hollywood are immortalized, now contains more than 2,500 five-pointed terrazzo and brass stars? I have yet to be nominated for such a plaque on the sidewalks of Hollywood Boulevard or Vine Street, but I did receive a star on the Bammies Walk of Fame in San Francisco. Only eight other musicians have been honored this way, including Carlos Santana, Jerry Garcia, Journey, and Jefferson Starship. Tourist attractions aside, I can sure drink like the movie stars. Ha! Whether you're throwing an award night bash, hosting your next movie night, or just want to add some star power to your cocktail party up in the Hollywood Hills, the Higher Spirit will take you there. It features a glorious trio of mezquila, aperol, and yellow chartreuse. Add a little lime and agave, then dress up your glass with a grapefruit peel. I tell ya, serve these elegant sippers at your next stylish event and you'll have created the hottest ticket in town.

1 ounce Santo Mezquila

¾ ounce Aperol

½ ounce yellow chartreuse

¾ ounce fresh lime juice

¼ ounce agave nectar

GARNISH:
Long thin fresh
grapefruit peel

Fill a cocktail shaker with ice. Add the mezquila, Aperol, yellow chartreuse, lime juice, and agave nectar. Shake well and double strain into a chilled coupe glass. Garnish with a long, thin fresh grapefruit peel.

HOT TIKI TODDY

As I'm sure you've discovered by now, I enjoy adding curveballs to the classics. I find they invigorate the drinks while making them stand out from the norm. Here's another one of my Tinseltown twists: A tiki spin on the traditional hot toddy. It's also one of my go-to's when I'm performing and find myself under the weather. After a couple of these, it usually isn't long until I'm back on the top of my game—especially when I'm belting out tunes like "Oh Yeah," "Baby's On Fire," and "Whole Lotta Zep." If you're stirring up this Toddy to ward off a chill or temper a cold, or are just looking for a soothing beverage to relax with after a long night of partying with the A-listers, you'll appreciate how quickly it comes together. Try it with Meyer lemon if you can get your hands on them. They're smaller and less acidic than regular lemons, and they deliver a sweet yet tart lemon flavor without overpowering the other ingredients in the drink.

---

3 ounces Sammy's Beach
Bar Platinum Rum
(or Sammy's Beach Bar Kola
Spiced Rum)

4 tablespoons honey

3 tablespoons fresh
lemon juice

½ piece fresh lemon rind

1 dash (about 1/6 teaspoon)
nutmeg

6–8 ounces boiling water

GARNISH:
Cinnamon stick, anise,
fresh nutmeg

In a heavy glass or mug, add the rum, honey, fresh lemon juice, lemon rind, and nutmeg. Next, slowly add the boiling water. Stir all the ingredients with the cinnamon stick and keep the stick in the drink (if desired). Finish the garnish with anise and fresh nutmeg.

MOJITO RISING

If you're like me, I've always found the Academy Awards entertaining. From red-carpet interviews and extravagant fashions to acceptance speeches and the award parties that follow, it's fun to see the hottest contenders compete for the ultimate prize in the industry. So, when you're planning your night to celebrate Hollywood's finest, you need a cocktail that's just as Oscar-worthy. Pass around a silver tray loaded with these award-worthy eye-pleasers and you'll instantly become a star. I've found the best way to enjoy these delicious charmers is with family, friends, and a big screen TV. First, you'll muddle some fresh raspberries, mint, and lime. Then you'll blend two styles of rum before topping with soda water and garnishing to party perfection. It's a sweet romance for your taste buds. Just follow the easy recipe below and your Mojito Rising might just win Best Drink!

3 fresh raspberries

4–6 fresh mint leaves

¾ ounce fresh lime juice

1½ ounces Sammy's Beach Bar Platinum Rum

½ ounce Sammy's Beach Bar Red Head Rum

Soda water, as needed

GARNISH:
Fresh watermelon slice, lime wheel, mint sprig

In a cocktail shaker, add the raspberries, mint leaves, and lime juice. Using a muddler, gently (yet firmly) muddle the ingredients. Add both rums and shake lightly. Pour into a Collins glass filled with ice. Top with soda water and garnish with a slice of fresh watermelon, lime wheel, and mint sprig.

PEPPER UPPER

This drink is my riff on the Rum and Coke, but with Dr Pepper making a dazzling appearance. For those of you from Waco, Texas, you know Dr Pepper was born in your city and is the oldest major soft drink in the United States. Hell, you guys even have a Dr Pepper Museum commemorating the drink that was originally marketed as a brain tonic. Today, Dr Pepper is cherished all across the land, especially here in Hollywood, which has had a long love affair with the soda pop. Forrest Gump, Spider-Man, Short Circuit—they've all featured Dr Pepper in their films. It's also a key ingredient in one of my preferred drinks when performing in front of a packed house in L.A. Often, I'll knock back some shots with my band before carrying a Pepper Upper on stage with me. Haha! That's the way I roll! I tell ya, man, there's something about this cocktail. It's complicated and bubbly, with bittersweet notes of chocolate and molasses. If you're ready for a Texas-style Cuba Libre sans the lime, you gotta make one of these. There's definitely an extra zip thanks to the Doctor.

2 ounces Sammy's Beach Bar Platinum Rum

Dr Pepper, as needed

1 splash Sammy's Beach Bar Red Head Rum (optional)

GARNISH:
Fresh orange wedge and mint sprig

Fill a rocks or highball glass with ice. Add the rum and top with Dr Pepper. Stir well. Add a float of Sammy's Red Head Rum on top, if desired. Garnish with a fresh orange wedge and mint sprig.

RED SAINT

Forget the milk and cookies this Christmas. Roll out the red carpet for Jolly ol' Saint Nick with a Red Saint. After all, he's about to adorn your tree with presents. Hands down, this is one star-studded drink, and one I invented while confined to my house during the COVID-19 pandemic. The vibrant red color is festive while the flavors are built on tequila, rum, triple sec, and citrus. One taste and you'll want to curl up on the couch in front of a roaring fire while listening to "Santa's Going South for Christmas." I sang this as a duet with Nancy Wilson on her Heart & Friends Home for the Holidays *special. The Red Saint is my new drink during this time of year, and it's as synonymous with the holidays as the world-famous Hollywood sign is to Los Angeles. Let me know what you think of this delicious, yet powerful concoction (you'll want to sip, not gulp). Personally, it might be the best drink I've ever tasted—truth.*

1 or 2 ounces Santo Blanco Tequila

½ ounce Sammy's Beach Bar Platinum Rum

½ ounce Sammy's Beach Bar Red Head Rum

1 ounce fresh lime juice

½ ounce triple sec (or any high-quality orange liqueur)

½ ounce fresh tangerine juice with peel, optional

RIM:
Vanilla extract and sugar and cinnamon (equal amounts mixed together) with a touch of nutmeg

GARNISH:
Fresh tangerine slice and cinnamon stick

Dip the rim of a chilled martini glass in some vanilla extract and roll the moistened rim in the sugar, cinnamon, and nutmeg mixture. Set the glass aside. In a cocktail shaker filled with ice, add the tequila, both rums, lime juice, triple sec, and the tangerine juice and peel, if using. Shake well (about 16 to 20 shakes) and strain into the prepared glass. Garnish with a fresh tangerine slice and cinnamon stick.

SKINNY RITA

When it comes to staying fit, few people know how to do it better than Hollywood's famous. Many celebrities follow strict and unique or unusual diets accompanied by intense workout routines. If you're after a refreshing and satisfying cocktail to shed the calories, but not the taste, make one of my Skinny Ritas. For me, this drink makes me think—not of weight loss or the gym—but of sunny, relaxed afternoons outside my California home, of long vacations, and warm beaches where I like digging my toes into the sand. I never get tired of those feelings, and I certainly never tire of a well-made margarita—even if it is low-cal. The secret to this margarita is skipping the orange liqueur and replacing it with citrus and agave nectar. I also like my margarita to bite me back, so I lean heavier on the lime juice and lighter on the nectar. Party on when you raise this famous Hollywood-inspired cocktail.

2 ounces Cabo Wabo Blanco Tequila

¾ ounce agave nectar

1 fresh lime, cut in half

Soda water, as needed

RIM:
Fresh lime and sea salt

Run a fresh lime wedge around the rim of an old fashioned or rocks glass. Then roll the moistened rim in sea salt and set the glass aside. Next, add the tequila and agave nectar to a shaker filled with ice. Squeeze the juice from both halves of the lime into the shaker and drop one of the squeezed lime halves into the shaker (discarding the other half). Shake well and pour the entire contents into the prepared glass. Top with soda water.

SOUTH-OF-THE-BORDER OLD FASHIONED

Some bourbon, sugar, bitters, and a twist, the Old Fashioned has always been a dependable formula; a simple architecture that has stood firm in drinking history for centuries. But when I want a Cabo Wabo spin on this vintage sipper, I turn to tequila. Featured as yet another one of our Hollywood drink menu specialties, the South-of-the-Border shines when tequila takes center stage. Combined with bitters and agave nectar (rather than sugar), the result is nothing short of familiar, satisfying, and delicious. I don't know about you, but to me, a Mexican cocktail without citrus is not a Mexican cocktail. That's why I like to add a little muddled lime and orange. I find the citrus freshens up the drink and takes it to a higher level. Next time you're feeling like a riff on an ol' classic, throw on Montrose's "Rock Candy" and stir up one of these hard and sweet babies.

2 fresh lime wedges

1 fresh orange wedge

2 ounces Hornitos Black Barrel Añejo Tequila

¾ ounce agave nectar

2 dashes Angostura bitters

GARNISH:
Maraschino cherry

Add the orange and two lime wedges to an old fashioned or rocks glass. Using a muddler, gently (yet firmly) muddle the ingredients and fill the shaker with ice. Add the tequila, agave nectar, and bitters. Stir well and garnish with a maraschino cherry.

SOUTHBOUND GREYHOUND

SERVES 1

A classic in itself, this fabulous-tasting cocktail is another that makes my Greatest Hits list because it's made with Deep Eddy Vodka, which is inspired by the oldest swimming hole in Austin, Texas. A place where people come together to enjoy good times that never seem to end. That's also the vibe and motto at Cabo Wabo Hollywood where this drink reigns supreme. California happens to be the place where my family and I hole up for most of the year, and where I rehearse with my band and do shows in L.A. What's also cool about this cocktail, which I often sip backstage after performing in Tinseltown, is that you don't need a cocktail shaker to enjoy it. Just pour over ice, splash in some grapefruit and soda, and share with friends or bandmates. It's that abiding, appetizing, and versatile.

2 ounces Deep Eddy
Ruby Red Vodka

1 ounce Simple Syrup
(page 233)

2 ounces fresh ruby red
grapefruit juice

Soda water, as needed

GARNISH:
Fresh lime wheel

Add the vodka, Simple Syrup, and grapefruit juice to a cocktail shaker filled with ice. Shake well and pour the entire contents into an old fashioned or rocks glass. Top with soda water and garnish with a fresh lime wheel.

STRAWBERRY SURF

Surf's always up here in California, especially with this Cabo Wabo Hollywood special. The Strawberry Surf is a fruity cocktail lover's dream that's not too sweet and not too heavy. Part mojito, part daiquiri, the sweetness of fresh, muddled strawberry makes this the ideal drink for your next California beach party. In 2020, when I relocated my annual Birthday Bash from Cabo Wabo Cantina in Mexico to the historic shores of exotic Catalina Island, California, I made sure these refreshing cocktails made the drink list. After performing with The Circle and fellow Rock 'n' Roll Hall of Famers Michael Anthony, Jason Bonham, and Vic Johnson, we all toasted with a Red Rocker (page 176) and a Strawberry Surf. I watched as my bands lit up on the first sip of the Surf. "No, really, this is the best summer cocktail I've ever had!" they said. It was just what I wanted to hear, and not just because it was my birthday. These sippers are really magical. One of the best parts about this cocktail is that you can control the sweetness and alcohol content of each drink. Like them fruity? Add more strawberry. Like them boozy? Add more rum. Personally, I like my Strawberry Surfs lightly sweet with plenty of rum.

3 fresh strawberries, hulled

½ ounce fresh lime juice

1½ ounces Sammy's Beach Bar Platinum Rum

3 ounces Sweet & Sour Mix (page 235)

¾ ounce Strawberry Purée (page 232)

GARNISH:
Fresh lime wheel

Add the strawberries and lime juice to a cocktail shaker. Using a muddler, gently (yet firmly) muddle the ingredients and fill the shaker with ice. Add the rum, Sweet & Sour Mix, and Strawberry Purée. Shake well and pour the entire contents into an old fashioned or rocks glass. Garnish with a fresh lime wheel.

SUMMER SPLASH

The next time you're ready to craft cocktails for another Hollywood at-home movie party, include the Summer Splash, which I give the silver-screen stamp of approval. I promise your guests will feel like 1940s Tinseltown starlets when they sip this effervescent classic. A riff on the Screwdriver, the Summer Splash is all attitude and glamour with a touch of cinematic magic: Two parts rum to two parts orange juice, and a mingle of tonic for the fizz. It's a simple, clean, memorable drink—just like the ending of the film Casablanca. *The orange wheel garnish also perks up the glass with that tropical Moroccan flair.*

2 ounces Sammy's
Beach Bar Rum

2 ounces fresh orange juice

Tonic water, as needed

GARNISH:
Fresh orange wheel

Fill a Collins glass with ice. Add the rum and orange juice. Stir well and top with tonic water. Garnish with a fresh orange wheel.

SWEET HITCHHIKER

When I think about movies and cocktails, James Bond and his vodka martini—shaken, not stirred—always come to mind. But let's not forget the scene when Bond orders a rum and soda at the Ocean Club in the Bahamas in Casino Royale. *As a devoted rummy, I enjoyed a fist pump when I saw that my favorite super spy was finally off the vodka and on to the rum! This Sweet Hitchhiker is a delicious cocktail laden with rum, cola, and more rum, then kissed with a wedge of fresh lime. It's bliss and beauty in its simplest form, especially on a hot summer night with—what else—"Summer Nights" wafting through the air. I'll admit, this lick is one of personal favorites from my days with Van Halen. In the song, I sing about partying it up while Michael Anthony's sunny vocals echo in the background. When you hear it, you'll want to fill your glass with ice and make a Sweet Hitchhiker. Can you say "instant party"?*

1 ounce Sammy's Beach Bar
Kola Spiced Rum

6 ounces Coca-Cola

1 ounce Sammy's Beach Bar
Red Head Rum

GARNISH:
Fresh lime wedge

Fill a rocks glass with ice. Add the spiced rum and cola. Stir well and float the Red Head Rum on top. Garnish with a fresh lime wedge.

SAMMY'S CALIENTE
MARGARITA

WATERMELON JALAPEÑO
MARGARITA

AÑEJO RITUAL

F' ME GINGER

RED HEAD SCORPION

SERIOUS PINEAPPLE JUJU

SAMMY HA
COCKTAIL

SIDE 1

2. SAMMY'S "VELVET KICKSTAND" MARGARITA
1. RED HEAD MAI TAI
3. WAKE UP SCREAMING
4. WABORITA & WABO POP
5. LITTLE RED DEVIL
6. JALAPENO CABO KISS

THERE'S NO SUCH THING AS A GREAT ROCK SHOW THAT DOESN'T END WITH AN ENCORE—WHICH IS JUST FINE WITH ME. There's no better feeling than walking onstage, playing and singing my heart out for two hours, giving it everything I've got, then hearing the fans stomp and yell and scream for even more. I crave that sweat-drenched, sore throat, party-all-night energy almost as much as I crave great tequila and rum. So, it's no mystery why this tasting tour of my favorite cocktails ends the same way I like to close the last live show on a worldwide tour—with a few more of the hits that brought you here in the first place.

This short list of cocktails features two new tequilas created with my good friend Guy Fieri plus a pineapple rum to make all your tropical dreams come true. My advice? Flip to this chapter anytime you want to make last call last all night.

Reposado and Añejo were the natural choices when Guy and I decided to expand our tequila line. We started with the pure blue agave taste of Santo Blanco Tequila and aged each differently and both to perfection. The Reposado spent just a few months in once-used whisky barrels. Guy and I tasted, kept tasting, and tasted some more—waiting for the peak flavor we were after. The result? A round, soft flavor profile with enough oak to elevate the tequila, but not so much that it overpowers the other ingredients in your top-shelf cocktails. Try the pineapple jalapeño combo in my Caliente Margarita or the refreshingly sweet Watermelon Jalapeno Margarita. Make a pitcher if you want to. String up your hammock and wait for the vacation to come to you.

After we tasted our Reposado, Guy and I decided to keep on going, handcrafting an Añejo—a tequila made for sipping, not shooting. Ours is aged for twelve to eighteen months in the same once-used whisky barrels we use for the Reposado. It's smooth, warm, and sultry, like an amber sunset swirling in your glass. It's meant to be enjoyed the same way you'd drink a brandy: neat, at room temperature, with a cigar if that's your thing. But for something entirely unexpected, serve it in a wine glass rimmed with cinnamon, garnished with a thin slice of orange. I call it the Añejo Ritual, because it's a drink that bears repeating.

Each barrel-aged bottle of our Añejo varies slightly in flavor and gets the same level of attention I give to my music and Guy gives to his dishes. One taste will tell you: we're hands on, we're perfectionists, and we don't cut corners.

If your sipping tastes are more rum-based, you'll love the refreshingly sweet pineapple rum I've added to my Sammy's Beach Bar Rum collection. It's a lower proof than my other rums—55 to be exact. What can I say? It's my number. And in this case, it's a sweet one. Pour this charmer over ice with a fresh mint sprig and lime slice and you've got a drink I call Serious Pineapple Juju. For a little more sting, try a brandy-coated Red Head Scorpion, my take on a cocktail that—if the rumors are true—crashed its first party in

1930s Honolulu. For good measure, I threw in a third recipe that's as colorful as its name, the F' Me Ginger.

And that, my friends, brings us to the end of our transcontinental cocktail tour. I hope I showed you a few new things, introduced you to some new flavors, and gave you a taste of the Cabo Wabo way of life. It's served me well, and my hope is that these cocktails do the same for you.

Take good care, Redheads.

Here's to love and friendship.

Here's to you.

SAMMY'S CALIENTE MARGARITA

This is my version of a Caliente Margarita—fitting for a warm spring night or a Cinco de Mayo soirée. Tequila partner Guy Fieri created a similar margarita for our Santo Spirit tequila-mezquila line. This marg, made with our Reposado, is equally fresh, simple, and delicious. The aged tequila is the perfect canvas for the tropical juices and agave that makes this drink come alive. When creating this cocktail, I stuck to the traditional base of tequila and lime while substituting the orange liquor with homemade agave simple syrup and adding a boost of flavor and kick with jalapeño, cilantro, and pineapple. I tell ya, man, after a few sips of this Mexican favorite, everything seems to be right in the world.

1 thin slice fresh jalapeño

5–6 fresh cilantro sprigs

2 ounces Santo Reposado Tequila

1 ounce Agave Simple Syrup (page 233)

¾ ounce fresh lime juice

¾ ounce fresh pineapple juice

GARNISH:
Fresh lime wheel

In a clean, dry cocktail shaker, add the slice of jalapeño and the cilantro. Using a muddler, gently (yet firmly) muddle the ingredients and fill the shaker with ice. Add the tequila, Agave Simple Syrup, lime juice, and pineapple juice. Shake hard and strain into a chilled margarita or coupe glass filled with ice and garnish with a fresh lime wheel.

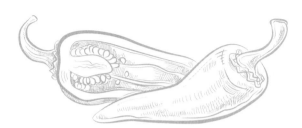

WATERMELON JALAPEÑO MARGARITA

Here's another savory tequila cocktail you gotta try. I made this with Guy Fieri as a Valentine's Day special for our fans. It also features our Reposado. The drink comes together quickly using everyday ingredients, and it's pretty to look at, too. Man, the vibrant color just screams love. Thanks to the watermelon, the cocktail has a naturally sweet flavor. Mix up a batch and pass them around. The combination of tequila, watermelon, Sweet & Sour, and orange will wake up your taste buds and make them say—"Let's get this weekend started!"

1½ ounces (or more) Santo Reposado Tequila

2 ounces Watermelon Syrup (page 234)

2 ounces Sweet & Sour Mix (page 235)

½ ounce fresh orange juice

GARNISH:
Fresh watermelon wedge and jalapeño slice

In a cocktail shaker filled with ice, add the tequila, Watermelon Syrup, Sweet & Sour Mix, and orange juice. Strain into a chilled rocks glass or brandy snifter filled with ice. Garnish with a fresh watermelon wedge and jalapeño slice.

AÑEJO RITUAL

SERVES
1

I enjoy sipping Añejos neat and at room temperature. But sometimes the old-world flavors of this tequila are deserving of the age-old ritual: a pinch of spice, tequila, followed with a taste of citrus. While most tequilas are served up with a lick of finely ground salt (to help temper the burn of the spirit) and a bite of limón (masks or enhances the tequila flavor, depending on who you ask), I prefer another flavor combination. I replace the salt with cinnamon and substitute the Mexican lime with an orange slice or wedge. I call this the Añejo Ritual, and I'll serve it in a small champagne flute or small white wine glass. That's because Añejos should be treated like a fine brandy, scotch, or rum. That means I'll nose it gently with small sips while allowing the flavors to open up. The best atmosphere to enjoy this liquid treat is in a relaxed setting with family or the closest of friends.

1½ ounces (or more) Santa
Añejo Tequila

RIM:
Orange and ground
cinnamon

GARNISH:
Fresh orange wedge
or wheel

Run an orange wedge around the rim of a small champagne flute or small white wine glass. Then roll the moistened rim in ground cinnamon. Next, add the tequila, and garnish with a wedge or wheel of fresh orange.

F' ME GINGER

"Shiver me timbers!" pirates would holler as a large wave or cannonball smashed into their sailing ship, shuddering the hull and splintering the timbers into oblivion. "F' Me Ginger!" is what you'll holler (Gin-ja if you use your best sailor voice) when you take a sip of this absolutely delicious concoction. It's the first drink I developed that marries my pineapple and macadamia rums, which I further elevate with fresh tropical juices—like the ol' seafarers would have done. This fruity cocktail, with a snap of flavor thanks to the zing of freshly grated ginger, is perfect for opening days on the boat or perched right next to your sun lounger beside the pool.

1 ounce Sammy's Beach Bar Pineapple Rum (or 1½ ounces Sammy's Beach Bar Platinum Rum muddled with 1 large slice fresh pineapple and strained)

½ ounce Sammy's Red Head Rum

½ ounce triple sec

½ ounce fresh lime juice

1 ounce fresh orange juice

1 teaspoon finely grated fresh ginger root

RIM:
Vanilla extract and ground cinnamon (or a mixture of ground cinnamon and powdered sugar)

GARNISH:
Fresh mint sprig

Dip the rim of a chilled martini glass in some vanilla extract then roll the moistened rim in ground cinnamon. Set the glass aside. In a cocktail shaker filled with ice, add the pineapple rum, Red Head Rum, triple sec, lime juice, orange juice, and ginger. Shake for at least 30 seconds to infuse the flavor of the ginger. Strain into the prepared martini glass and garnish with a fresh mint sprig. **Note:** For a lighter version, strain into a Collins glass filled with ice and top with soda water.

RED HEAD SCORPION

Based on an original drink by Trader Vic, the individually sized Scorpion has been adapted by bartenders across the globe for the last seventy years. Similar to our Wabo Bowl (page 166), I can't get enough of this fresh, tart, and lightly sweetened mixture that's nicely spiked with the pleasant sensation of pineapple rum, Red Head Rum, and brandy. The result is a year-round cocktail that I find rich and delicious with layer upon layer of aroma and flavor. This tiki-inspired drink also garnishes well. I like adding a slice of orange and a fresh mint sprig but have some fun with the accoutrements by including edible flowers, pineapple wedges, cherries, and other citrus. You can also increase the measurements and turn this tropical punch into a boozy bowl complete with straws for you and your friends.

1½ ounces Sammy's Beach Bar Pineapple Rum

¾ ounce brandy or cognac

½ ounce orgeat syrup

2 ounces fresh orange juice

1 ounce fresh lemon juice

Drizzle of Sammy's Red Head Rum

GARNISH:
Fresh orange slice and mint sprig

In a kitchen or bar blender, add the pineapple rum, brandy, orgeat syrup, and orange and lemon juices. Add a scoop of ice and blend until smooth. Pour into a Collins glass and drizzle a little of Sammy's Red Head Rum over the top. Garnish with a fresh orange slice and mint sprig.

SERIOUS PINEAPPLE JUJU

SERVES
1

In Charles Dickens's Pickwick Papers—*about the joys of travel and the pleasures of eating and drinking well—Reverend Stiggins boasts of his favorite beverage: pineapple rum. Dating back to the 1700s, pineapple rum has been appreciated by many the world over, especially those in the Caribbean, where fresh pineapples were often soaked in rum barrels. Today, this love affair between spirits and tropical fruit hasn't wavered. Following similar techniques of those island rum producers, I find that fermentation, distillation, and blending of my pineapple rum creates a rich, fruity spirit that's ideal for mixed drinks or on its own, which I refer to as a glass of Serious Pineapple Juju. Enjoy this smooth, exotic rum over ice while jamming to my track "Serious Juju." You Redheads know the words: "Don't disturb my paradise. I've asked you once, I asked you nice. Mother Earth will punish you. With some serious juju." In this case, the serious juju is a glass of—what else—pineapple rum.*

1 fresh mint sprig

1½ ounces (or more) Sammy's Beach Bar Pineapple Rum

GARNISH:
Fresh lime slice

First, bruise the mint sprig to release the fragrant oils. Do this by simply crushing the leaves in your hand or sticking the mint in a bag and whacking it a couple time with a wooden spoon. Now add a little ice to a small white wine glass and add the mint followed by the rum. Garnish with a fresh lime slice.

Cocktail Foundations

(Homemade Purées, Syrups, Mixers, and Salts)

BLOOD ORANGE PURÉE

MAKES ABOUT ¾ CUP

4 whole blood oranges, peeled, segmented, and seeded

2 tablespoons Simple Syrup (page 233)

1 teaspoon lemon juice

In a bar or kitchen blender, add the oranges, Simple Syrup, and lemon juice. Blend until smooth and puréed. Add more or less Simple Syrup and lemon juice to achieve your desired taste. Store in an airtight container in the refrigerator until needed. Lasts about 1 week.

MANGO PURÉE

MAKES ABOUT 3 CUPS

2 ripe mangos, peeled, pitted, and sliced into chunks

⅓ cup sugar

2 tablespoons water

In a kitchen blender, add the mango, sugar, and water. Purée until smooth. Reserve until ready to use.

PEACH PURÉE

MAKES ABOUT 2 CUPS

1¼ pound fresh diced peaches (from about 3 peaches)

1½ ounces water

½ ounce fresh lemon juice

Sugar, as needed

Using a kitchen or immersion blender, add the diced peaches, water and lemon juice. Blend until smooth. Taste and add sugar, up to 3 tablespoons, depending on sweetness of peaches. Blend to incorporate and then set the purée aside until ready to use. This purée will last about three days in the refrigerator or three months in the freezer.

STRAWBERRY PURÉE

MAKES ABOUT 1¼ CUPS

¾ pound fresh strawberries, washed, hulled, and quartered

Sugar, as needed, optional

Place the strawberries in a pan and simmer over very low heat for about 15 minutes, or until the strawberries are broken down (this process enhances the flavor). Remove from pan and let cool. Add the berries to a bar or kitchen blender, and blend until smooth and puréed. You can add a little sugar if you feel the strawberries aren't sweet enough; usually between 1 teaspoon and 1 tablespoon, depending on the berries and how sweet you'd like the purée to be. Store in an airtight container in the refrigerator until needed. Lasts about 1 week.

AGAVE SIMPLE SYRUP

1 cup water
1 cup agave nectar

In a saucepan over low heat, add the water and agave nectar. Allow to simmer, stirring occasionally, until the nectar dissolves. Remove from heat. Once it has cooled, transfer to an airtight container and store in the refrigerator until ready to use. The syrup will last about one month.

HONEY SYRUP

1 cup honey
1 cup water

In a medium saucepan over medium heat, add the honey and water. Bring to a boil, stirring often, until the honey has dissolved. Allow to cool before storing in an airtight container in the refrigerator. Will keep for about one month.

LYCHEE SIMPLE SYRUP

1 cup sugar
1 cup water
1¼ cups peeled, seeded lychee (about 8 ounces whole fruit)

In a medium saucepan over medium heat, add the sugar, water, and lychee. Bring to a boil, stirring often, until the sugar has dissolved. Then lower to a simmer until the lychee is tender, about 10 minutes. Remove from heat, cover, and allow to cool for 10 to 15 minutes. Strain into an airtight container. Store in the refrigerator until ready to use. Will keep for about one month.

SIMPLE SYRUP

1 cup sugar
1 cup water

In a medium saucepan over medium heat, add the sugar and water. Bring to a boil, stirring often, until the sugar has dissolved. Remove from heat, cover, and allow to cool for 10 to 15 minutes. Store in the refrigerator until ready to use. Will keep for about one month.

STRAWBERRY SYRUP

MAKES ABOUT 2 CUPS

1½ cups (8 ounces) fresh strawberries, stems removed, sliced

1 cup sugar

1 cup water

Using a muddler, gently (yet firmly) muddle the strawberries. In a medium saucepan over medium heat, add the sugar, water, and muddled strawberries. Bring to a boil, stirring often, until the sugar has dissolved. Then lower to a simmer and allow the berries to further break down while the syrup turns a deep red, about 20 minutes. Remove from heat, cover, and allow the syrup to cool for 10 to 15 minutes. Double strain the syrup into an airtight container. Store in the refrigerator until ready to use. Will keep for about 2 weeks.

WATERMELON SYRUP

MAKES ABOUT 2 CUPS

½ large seedless watermelon (to yield 4 cups pureed watermelon)

1 cup sugar (brown sugar if you like your syrup extra rich)

Remove the rind from the watermelon and chop up the flesh. Add to a bar or kitchen blender, and blend until smooth. Strain the liquid (about 4 cups) into a saucepan and stir in the sugar. Place over medium heat and allow to simmer, stirring occasionally, until reduced by half (about 35 minutes, up to an hour). The longer you let it simmer, the thicker the syrup will be; just don't burn it; lower the heat if you need to. Remove from heat and allow to cool. Store in an airtight container in the refrigerator until ready to use. Lasts about 5 days.

LYCHEE JUICE

MAKES ABOUT 2 CUPS

30 pitted and peeled lychee fruit

1 cup water

2 tablespoons Simple Syrup (page 233)

Add the lychee and water into a bar or kitchen blender. Blend until smooth. Pass through a strainer, discarding the pulp. Combine the strained lychee with the Simple Syrup and mix well. Store in an airtight container in the refrigerator until ready to use. Will last about one week.

SWEET & SOUR MIX

1½ cups sugar

1½ cups water

1 cup fresh lime juice (8 to 10 medium limes)

1 cup fresh lemon juice (4 or 5 large lemons)

In a saucepan over low heat, add the sugar and water, and stir to combine. Allow to simmer over the heat until the sugar has completely dissolved. Remove from heat, transfer to an airtight container (like a Mason jar) and allow to cool. Once cool, add the lemon and lime juice, and mix or shake well to combine. Store in the refrigerator until ready to use. Will last for about one week.

CHIPOTLE SEA SALT

½ cup sea salt

¾ teaspoon chipotle powder

Add the salt and chipotle powder to a small container with a lid. Seal the container and shake until the salt and chipotle powder are well combined. Store until ready to use; the salt will keep indefinitely.

SAMMY'S SEA SALT

1 gallon Cabo San Lucas seawater (or other pure, pristine oceanwater)

Pour the seawater in a large pot over high heat and bring to a boil. Allow to boil for 10 minutes to kill any bacteria. Remove from heat and carefully pour the boiled seawater ½ inch deep in a shallow, nonreactive baking sheet or glass Pyrex dish. Cover with cheese-cloth and set in the hot sun until the liquid has evaporated (be patient; this can take anywhere from several days to one week). Consolidate the salt on the sheet and place in a warm, dry area (like the oven) overnight to completely dry. Transfer the salt to an airtight jar and store until ready to use.

BACKSTAGE PRAISE

The authors would like to thank the following individuals for all their help and support with this book:

Manager Tom Consolo for connecting James and Sammy and helping to push this book through; Stan Novack for wrangling the recipes; Nicole Hardy for her literary assistance; Cocktail photographers, stylists, and recipe testers Jeff Tucker and Kevin Hossler of Tucker + Hossler Photography; Lifestyle photographer Leah Steiger; Book designer Jen Montgomery; Cover designer Todd Gallopo of Meat + Potatoes; Nicole Frail, Abigail Gehring, and the entire team at Skyhorse Publishing; Everyone behind the scenes at Cabo Wabo Cantinas, Sammy's Beach Bar & Grills, Sammy's Beach Bar Rum and Santo Spirit; Guy Fieri; Renata Ravina; Kari Hagar and the Hagar Family; Tiffany Fraioli.

Sammy would like to personally thank:

Grupo Campari for watching over my first child, Cabo Wabo Tequila, and their generous support of the Cantinas.

All of my longtime friends and supporters of my brands at Southern Glazer's Wine & Spirits. It's nice to be part of the family.

My band the Circle, Jason, Mikey, and Vic, for being not just my favorite band in the world, but dear friends.

All those bartenders and mixologists out there who care enough about their reputation to take the time to make great cocktails for all of us to enjoy.

All of my chef friends for supporting my spirit brands and for keeping my tummy full of yummy.

Last, but certainly not least, the Redheads— the fans—who have been following me through all of my crazy, fun, and wacky adventures. Without you, I wouldn't be living this wonderful life. Thank you from the bottom of my heart. I am eternally and gratefully at your service.

INDEX

Standard Conversions

METRIC AND IMPERIAL CONVERSIONS

(These conversions are rounded for convenience)

Ingredient	Cups/ Tablespoons/ Teaspoons	Ounces	Grams/Milliliters
Fruit, dried	1 cup	4 ounces	120 grams
Fruits or veggies, chopped	1 cup	5 to 7 ounces	145 to 200 grams
Fruits or veggies, puréed	1 cup	8.5 ounces	245 grams
Honey, maple syrup, or corn syrup	1 tablespoon	0.75 ounce	20 grams
Liquids: cream, milk, water, or juice	1 cup	8 fluid ounces	240 milliliters
Salt	1 teaspoon	0.2 ounces	6 grams
Spices: cinnamon, cloves, ginger, or nutmeg (ground)	1 teaspoon	0.2 ounce	5 milliliters
Sugar, brown, firmly packed	1 cup	7 ounces	200 grams
Sugar, white	1 cup/1 tablespoon	7 ounces/0.5 ounce	200 grams/12.5 grams
Vanilla extract	1 teaspoon	0.2 ounce	4 grams

LIQUIDS

8 fluid ounces = 1 cup = ½ pint

16 fluid ounces = 2 cups = 1 pint

32 fluid ounces = 4 cups = 1 quart

128 fluid ounces = 16 cups = 1 gallon